PHILIP LARKIN

PHILIP LARKIN

PHILIP LARKIN

Laurence Lerner

Second Edition

NORTHCOTE
BRITISH COUNCIL

© Copyright 1997 and 2005 by Laurence Lerner

First published in 1997 by Northcote House Publishers Ltd, Horndon, Tavistock, Devon, PL19 9NQ, United Kingdom.
Tel: +44 (0) 1822 810066 Fax: +44 (0) 1822 810034.

Second edition 2005

British Library Cataloguing-in-Publication Data
A catalogue record for this book is available from the British Library

ISBN 0 7463 1137 0

Typeset by PDQ Typesetting, Newcastle-under-Lyme
Printed and bound in the United Kingdom by Baskerville Press Ltd, Salisbury

'I should hate anybody to read my work because he's been told to, and told what to think about it.'

Philip Larkin, *Required Writing*

Contents

Acknowledgements

Quotations from the Larkin Archive are by permission of the trustees; those from *The Less Deceived* by permission of the Marvell Press, and all other quotations by permission of Faber & Faber Ltd. in England, and Farrar, Strauss & Giroux Inc. in the USA.

Biographical Outline

1922	Born in Coventry, second child and only son of Sydney (the City Treasurer) and his wife Eva.
1932–40	King Henry VIII School, Coventry.
1940	Enters St John's College, Oxford, to study English Literature.
1943	Graduates with first class honours. In December, appointed librarian at Wellington, Shropshire.
1945	*The North Ship* published by Fortune Press.
1946	Appointed assistant librarian at University College, Leicester. *Jill* published by Fortune Press.
1947	*A Girl in Winter* published by Faber & Faber.
1948	Death of his father. Fails to find a publisher for his collection *In the Grip of Light*.
1950	Appointed sub-librarian at Queen's University, Belfast.
1951	*XX Poems* privately printed.
1954	Fantasy Poets No. 21 (a pamphlet of five poems) published by Fantasy Press, Oxford.
1955	Appointed librarian at the University of Hull. *The Less Deceived* published by Marvell Press, Hull.
1956	*New Lines*, edited by Robert Conquest, published by Macmillan.
1963	*New Lines* 2 published.
1964	*The Whitsun Weddings* published by Faber & Faber.
1965	Awarded the Queen's Gold Medal for Poetry.
1970	*All What Jazz* published by Faber & Faber.
1970–1	Visiting Fellow, All Soul's College, Oxford.
1973	*The Oxford Book of Twentieth-Century English Verse* published by Clarendon Press, Oxford.

1974	*High Windows* published by Faber & Faber.
1975	Made CBE (Companion of the British Empire).
1976	Receives the Shakespeare prize in Hamburg.
1977	Death of his mother.
1978	Made Companion of Literature by the Royal Society of Literature.
1983	*Required Writing* published by Faber & Faber.
1984	Hon. D.Litt., Oxford University (his seventh honorary degree). Offered, but refused, the office of Poet Laureate on the death of John Betjeman.
1985	Made CH (Companion of Honour). Illness and death.

Abbreviations and References

Archive The Philip Larkin Archive in the Brynmor Jones Library, University of Hull

CP *Collected Poems*, ed. Anthony Thwaite (London: Faber & Faber and the Marvell Press, 1988)

GW *A Girl in Winter* (London: Faber & Faber, 1947)

Jill *Jill* (2nd edn, London: Faber & Faber, 1975)

Life Andrew Motion, *Philip Larkin: A Writer's Life* (London: Faber & Faber, 1993)

RW *Required Writing: Miscellaneous Pieces 1955–1982* (London: Faber & Faber, 1983)

SL *Selected Letters of Philip Larkin 1940–1985*, ed. Anthony Thwaite (London: Faber & Faber, 1992)

1

The Life

Philip Larkin, poet and librarian, led an uneventful life. He never married, he virtually never went abroad, and he disliked appearing in public: almost alone among post-war British poets, he gave no readings of his work, and the rare occasions when he had to give a talk in public filled him with preparatory nervousness. His studiously ordinary and ordered life was shot through with a persistent melancholy: his letters are filled with remarks like 'I suddenly see myself as a freak and a failure, and my way of life as a farce. I suppose work normally shields one's eyes from home truths of this nature' (*SL* 329). Sometimes a melancholy wit enlivens such sentiments: 'I think autumn and winter are better than spring and summer in that they are not *supposed* to be enjoyable, isn't that it?' (*SL* 356). He had the reputation of a surly recluse, and did much to cultivate this, occasionally confessing ruefully that it was as much of a pose as making public appearances – only much pleasanter. Yet he had many friends, and most people who knew him found him thoughtful, gracious, and, on occasion, very funny. This depressive, worried, self-mocking personality is of interest to us because it belonged to the finest English poet of his time.

Larkin was born in 1922 in Coventry, where his father Sydney was City Treasurer. A deliberately unimpressive account of Coventry is given in his self-mocking poem 'I Remember, I Remember', which describes the places where his 'childhood was unspent' ('And here we have that splendid family | I never ran to when I got depressed'). He had one sister, ten years older, but said that he always felt like an only child. Some of his comments on his family are startling. 'Marriage seems a revolting institution,' he wrote when he was 21, 'unless the parties have enough money to keep reasonably distant from each other – imagine sharing a bedroom with a withered old woman.' There is, of course, something of a young man's bravado about this, but his scorn of family life, which he called 'an enormous absurdity', was deep and permanent: an autobiographical fragment which he wrote when he was about 30 describes his childhood as dominated by fear and boredom, and gives a bleak picture of his parents' marriage ('there was a curious tense boredom about the house'), claiming that it had left him with the conviction 'that human beings should not live together, and that children should be taken from their parents at an early age' (*Life*, 13–15). Yet when his father died he showed genuine grief and admiration: 'I felt very proud of him,' he wrote to a friend after the funeral; 'as my sister remarked afterwards, "we're nobody now, he did it all"' (*SL* 147); and he always defended his father's character staunchly, to the point of showing resentment against anyone who denigrated it. Towards his mother his attitude seems to have been deeply contradictory. Sometimes he wrote about her with unconcealed distaste: 'the monstrous whining monologues she treated my father to before breakfast, and all of us at meal-times, resentful, self-pitying, full of funk and suspicion, have remained in my mind as something I mustn't, *under any circumstances*, risk encountering again' (*Life*, 14). Yet he behaved like a loyal and devoted son, looking after her with great care during her long widowhood. Although he frequently described how bored he was by her company, and reproached himself for his irritation with her, those who knew him said he was devoted to her. This is one of the many paradoxes about Philip Larkin the man.

He was a good but not outstanding pupil at school, and left in 1940 to study English Literature ('What else?' he commented) at St John's College, Oxford. His whole career as a student was in wartime, yet the war made curiously little impression on him. 'Without being a conscientious objector,' he wrote, 'I did not want to join the Army on moral grounds. However I was fundamentally – like the rest of my friends – uninterested in the war' (Archive). Bad eyesight exempted him from war service, and he graduated in 1943. He wished to be a novelist, hoping 'to lead that wonderful five-hundred-words-a-day on-the-Riviera life that beckons us all like an *ignis fatuus* from the age of sixteen onwards' (*SL* 334) – and when interviewed for a post in the Civil

Service he said so, wondering wryly if his frankness had cost him the job); he had in the meantime to earn his living, and it was more or less by accident that he became a librarian. His first successful job application was for the post of librarian at Wellington, a small town in Shropshire, a post he had applied for without much interest, and entered on without enthusiasm. 'The library is a very small one,' he wrote; 'I am entirely unassisted in my labours, and spend most of my time handing out antiquated tripe to the lower levels of the general public' (*SL* 85). Although he made fun of his job, he worked at it conscientiously, and left the library in better condition than he found it. His move to the library of University College, Leicester, in 1946 meant that he was taking it seriously as a career; he took a diploma in librarianship in his spare time, moved to Queen's University, Belfast, as sub-librarian in 1950, and then in 1955 to Hull as university librarian, a post he held until his death. He planned and directed the building of a new library, and became a prominent figure in the world of university librarians, with a particular interest in the collecting and preservation of literary manuscripts.

Larkin's career as a poet had the same modest and provincial beginnings as his career as a librarian. In 1945 his first collection, *The North Ship*, came out from the Fortune Press, a small publisher mainly interested in pornography, who also published his novel *Jill* the following year; his second (and last) novel, *A Girl in Winter*, was published by Faber & Faber in 1947; what was to have been his second collection of poems, called *In the Grip of Light*, failed to find a publisher; he had a collection of *XX Poems* privately printed in 1951; a pamphlet of five poems was published by the Fantasy Press in 1954; and *The Less Deceived* by the Marvell Press, Hull, in 1955 – just before he came, coincidentally, to live in Hull. Together with occasional poems in periodicals, this is a record no different from dozens of other minor poets, known only to their friends and the enthusiastic readers of little magazines. The subsequent story is most encouraging for those who like to think that literary reputations are based on merit, not publicity. The Marvell Press was run on a shoestring by George and Jean Hartley, and they could not afford to launch the book (their first) with lavish advertising, but it received a number of enthusiastic reviews, and soon became a best-seller. The poetry magazine *Listen*, also published by the Hartleys, in which many of the poems had appeared, has become a collectors' piece; and Larkin became one of the best known poets in Britain. He was associated with what became known as the 'Movement', a group of poets, most of them university teachers, who stood for clarity, traditional forms, and reasonableness – in reaction immediately against the cloudy romanticism of the 1940s, most famously represented by Dylan Thomas, and more generally against the whole tendency of modernism. The manifesto of the Movement was Robert Conquest's introduction to *New Lines*, an anthology he edited in 1956 (followed by *New Lines 2* in 1963), in which he described the poets' 'refusal to abandon a rational structure and comprehensible language, even when the verse is most highly charged with sensuous or emotional intent'. This is an accurate description of Larkin's work, as it is of most of the other poets in the anthology: Elizabeth Jennings, John Holloway, Kingsley Amis, D. J. Enright, Conquest himself, and John Wain, but not of Thom Gunn and only partly of Donald Davie. The New Lines poets were not in fact a tight-knit group: only Conquest, Amis, and Wain were friends of Larkin's, and, as happens with most groups, they soon went their separate ways, but the grouping is not altogether misleading as an account of the poetry of the 1950s.

After *The Less Deceived* and *New Lines*, Larkin's career is a series of triumphs. His subsequent volumes were published by Faber & Faber, the leading poetry publishers in twentieth-century Britain; he was awarded the Queen's Gold Medal for Poetry in 1965; was invited to edit the *Oxford Book of Twentieth-Century English Verse*, and while working on it was a Visiting Fellow of All Soul's College; seven British universities awarded him honorary doctorates, culminating in Oxford in 1984; he was made a CBE in 1975 and a Companion of Honour in 1985; he received the Shakespeare Prize in Hamburg in 1976 (attending the ceremony was almost his only trip as an adult to what he sometimes called 'dirty abroad'); he was made a Companion of Literature by the Royal Society of Literature in 1978; and on the death of John Betjeman in 1984 he was offered, but refused, the office of Poet Laureate. He regarded this distinguished public career with the mixture of quiet pride and self-mockery that was so central to his character. Among literary people he made Hull famous, that region described in his poem 'Here', next to 'the widening river's slow presence', where 'domes and statues, spires and cranes cluster | Beside grain-scattered streets, barge-crowded water'. The Vice-Chancellor of the university, Brynmor Jones, with a kind of Larkinesque irony, would say 'I pay you a librarian's salary to write poems', but Larkin was valued by the university as a competent and hard-working librarian.

Larkin's fame made him only intermittently happy: it is clear from his letters, and from the testimonies of his friends, that his capacity for joy was very limited. Perhaps the deepest shadow over his last years was that he was no longer writing poetry. After the publication of *High Windows* in 1974 there were no more collections, and very few poems: during his last seven years he wrote only a few fragments and some doggerel verses to friends, and he was deeply distressed by this sterility. It was not a new feeling: in his late twenties he had written a piece called 'Writing about not Writing', in which he described

> the hangdog grin at the familiar question that progresses from *What are you writing now?* through *Are you writing anything now?* to *You write don't you?* and, finally, to silence, and the indissoluble conviction that with a little more industry, a little less self-indulgence, some tiny incalculable adjustment of forces already at one's command, one would have managed to trap in indestructible terms life as one had lived it... (Archive)

Larkin's knowledge that he did on occasion find these indestructible terms always had to contend with his fear of drying up, so that when the poetry really did dry up he found the experience especially painful. It combined at times with the fear of death, which in his case seems to have been unusually acute.

He died in 1985, two years before he was due to retire: he had dreaded retirement almost as much as he dreaded death.

2

The Novels

In the late 1940s, anyone who tried to predict Philip Larkin's career as a writer would have assumed that he would be a novelist. He had by then published two novels, the second with Faber & Faber, probably Britain's most prestigious literary publishers, and only one, rather derivative, volume of poems; his attempts to publish a second volume were meeting with no success. It was not until some years later that he finally abandoned his attempts at a third novel; and, as he was reluctantly obliged to give up fiction, he began to achieve success as a poet. Today, Larkin's novels are read mainly for the light they throw on his poetry, though both of them are worth reading for their own sake.

His development as a novelist was the reverse of his development as a poet. *Jill*, written in 1943–4, seems to belong to the realist movement of the 1950s, much concerned with class differences, and resembles the novels of John Braine, Kingsley Amis, and John Wain – the last two were friends of Larkin's, and closely associated with him as poets of the 'Movement'. *A Girl in Winter*, written a year later, is much more evocative, and reads more like the work of the early Larkin of *The North Ship*.

Jill is the story of John Kemp, a working-class boy from Lancashire who goes to Oxford in wartime and is faced with two contrasting (and hostile) worlds. They can be described as the world of those who eat carefully and that of those who eat carelessly (the novel is filled with vivid scenes of eating and drinking), and this difference is, of course, a matter of social class. On the one hand, there is Whitbread, like John a scholarship boy from the north of England, earnest and plodding, who works hard not because he likes studying (no one in the book is actually interested in his academic work), but with a calculating eye on career prospects; and, on the other, there is Warner, with whom John shares rooms, product of a minor public school, hard-drinking, coarse, and self-indulgent, who treats John with patronizing contempt. Whitbread has a scrupulous sense of property, whereas Warner steals food, borrows money, and breaks up other people's rooms. John finds that he dislikes Whitbread and longs to be accepted by Warner, whose rich insouciance arouses awe and envy in him (he does not at first realize that Warner is not really out of the top drawer socially, is neither as wealthy nor as aristocratic as he pretends). Larkin himself asserted, in the Preface to the reissue of the novel in 1963, that the book is not about class, and that his tendency at Oxford had been 'to minimise social differences rather than exaggerate them'; this may well be true of Larkin the man, but, in interpreting the novel, critics have accepted this disclaimer too readily. *Jill* (especially, but not only, in the first half) is dominated by questions of class. Many of the episodes recall the comic novels of Evelyn Waugh, perhaps the most class conscious of modern novelists: the scenes of undergraduate debauchery in *Decline and Fall* and *Brideshead Revisited* seem to provide a model for the destructive arrogance of Warner and his friends – so much so that the novel occasionally forgets that it is taking place during wartime austerity, and food and drink become as abundantly available as in the Oxford of the 1930s, in which Waugh's novels are set. Larkin is not as funny as Waugh, and is, of course, not interested in the theme of redemption with which Waugh, the Christian novelist, overlays his comedy. And the book does have another theme, at least as important as class: the relationship between fantasy and reality. Desperately trying to impress Warner, John invents a younger sister, Jill, who is at a boarding school called Willow Gables, and, although this catches Warner's attention for only a short time, John himself becomes obsessed by it: he writes (and posts!) letters to Jill, writes her replies, and starts to keep her diary, which is filled with the clichés of schoolgirl stories. Then one day, in a bookshop, he receives a shock: he sees Jill. This happens two-thirds of the way through the novel, and the remainder describes his efforts to get to know the girl who, he feels, 'is' Jill, and the disastrous results of his efforts to impose his fantasy on a real person.

A Girl in Winter is a complete contrast. It is carefully planned and written, with some exquisite wintry imagery which is clearly intended to symbolize withdrawal and isolation. Larkin himself described it as 'a pitiless book' that 'uses human beings to express an idea, rather than to express the truth about themselves' (*SL* 134). The first and last sections describe a day in the life of Katherine, a friendless wartime refugee, balanced between loneliness and self-sufficiency; the middle and longest section is a flashback to her pre-war visit to England to stay with the prosperous and friendly family of her penfriend Robin – three weeks of warm summer weather, in which the hoped-for intimacy with Robin had never quite developed.

A Girl in Winter feels like a highly original novel, although the influence of other novelists is very marked. The drab and hostile atmosphere in the library where Katherine works, and even more the visit to a bad-tempered dentist in a dingy surgery with a mended drill and dirty elbows to his white coat, obviously derive from Graham Greene. Less obvious, but more important, is the influence of Virginia Woolf, whose novels are pioneering works of modernism in the way they neglect the external events that traditionally provide a plot, in order to explore beneath the surface of what is said and done. Omission is central to the method of *A Girl in Winter*: not only are there striking omissions in the plot – we are never told what country Katherine is from (no actual country quite fits), or how she came to be in England during the war; there are more important difficulties when it comes to understanding her remarkable switches of mood. These switches constitute the most powerful and also the most unsatisfying elements in the novel:

> But once the break was made...life ceased to be a confused stumbling from one illumination to another, a series of unconnected clearings in a tropical forest, and became a flat landscape, wry and rather small, with a few unforgettable landmarks somewhat resembling a stretch of fenland, where an occasional dyke or broken fence shows up for miles, and the sails of a mill turn all day long in the steady wind.   (*GW* III. 2)

This step from the particular human situation to a generalizing simile, which then continues on its own momentum until it seems to have lost connection with the person or situation that prompted it, and becomes a reflection upon 'life', is a striking feature of Woolf's technique, which she sometimes uses to brilliant effect; its danger – as is very clear if we return this passage to its context – is that the simile can be used to conceal the author's own uncertainty about just what is going on.

Though so different in style and technique, the two novels do offer a similar view of life. Both end inconclusively, leaving us uncertain how, and even whether, the protagonist's problems are to be resolved.

> Then if there was no difference between love fulfilled and love unfulfilled, how could there be any difference between any other pair of opposites? Was he not freed, for the rest his life, from choice?   (*Jill*, 243)

This has the feel of a resolution, but John has learned nothing, and is as far as ever from finding his place in society. Katherine ends in a strikingly similar indifference, more powerfully rendered but just as negative:

> Unsatisfied dreams rose and fell about [the snowflakes], crying out against their implacability, but in the end glad that such order, such destiny, existed. Against this knowledge, the heart, the will, and all that made for protest, could at last sleep.   (*GW* III. 7)

We should perhaps remember that both novels are set in wartime, when the future is uncertain, and, as Robin remarks to Katherine, nothing seems to matter very much. But the theme of human relationships that never quite develop cannot be ascribed solely to the war: it is perhaps the most pervasive theme in all Larkin's writing, both in prose and poetry.

3

The Less Deceived

The early work of an important poet always has a potential interest, since it is likely to contain anticipations of his later, finer poems; in Larkin's case, however, this interest is limited because of the sharp break in his writing after *The North Ship*.

In 1943 Vernon Watkins came to speak at the Oxford English Club. Larkin was present, and the occasion made a tremendous and lasting impression on him. He never cared much for Watkins's own poems, but he liked the man tremendously, and responded to his enthusiasm for Dylan Thomas and, above all, for W. B. Yeats. 'Impassioned and imperative, he swamped us with Yeats...I had been tremendously impressed by the evening... As a result, I spent the next three years trying to write like Yeats, not because I liked his personality or understood his ideas, but out of infatuation with his music' (*RW* 29). Much of *The North Ship* almost sounds like a pastiche of Yeats: the poems have little to offer save a clearly derivative music. Not only are they thinner and less interesting than Larkin's mature work; they are arguably less interesting than some of his earlier poems, written when he was still an undergraduate, where the dominant influence is Auden (Auden surfaces again as an influence in the middle stanzas of 'The Building', thirty years later). Some of these early sonnets ('Conscript', 'A Writer', 'Observation') could be taken for Auden, whereas such *North Ship* poems as 'The moon is full tonight' or 'To write one song, I said' sound less like Yeats than like imitations of him: even the fact that they have no titles, when we realize how carefully chosen, and how important, the titles of Larkin's mature poems are, may be significant, suggesting that Larkin was quite right when he saw them as based on Yeat's music rather than his ideas.

10

By *XX Poems*, the privately printed volume in 1951, the mature Larkin has begun to appear; with *The Less Deceived* (which contained more than half of the *XX Poems*) he has clearly arrived. For many of Larkin's admirers, this remains his finest volume.

The book was originally called *Various Poems*, but George Hartley, when he accepted it for publication, objected to the feebleness of this, so Larkin renamed one of the poems 'Deceptions', and promoted its original title to the volume as a whole. Alerted by this, we can begin by looking at that poem, which is unusual among Larkin's work in that it tells someone else's story: beginning not from a personal experience but from a past event he has been reading about, in Henry Mayhew's pioneering work of interview journalism, *London Labour and the London Poor*, published in 1851. Mayhew's account of the young woman who was drugged, and discovered next morning that she had, in her nineteenth-century terminology, been 'ruined', and 'for some days was inconsolable, and cried like a child to be killed or sent back to my aunt', is deeply moving, and almost any modern reader will react by sympathizing with the victim: the first stanza of the poem, about her suffering ('Even so distant, I can taste the grief, | Bitter and sharp with stalks, he made you gulp') is the one most of us would think of writing. Then – unexpectedly, perhaps shockingly – the poem moves from the victim to the rapist, from her suffering to the deceptions of his desire.

> Slums, years, have buried you. I would not dare
> Console you if I could. What can be said,
> Except that suffering is exact, but where
> Desire takes charge, readings will grow erratic?
> For you would hardly care
> That you were less deceived, out on that bed,
> Than he was, stumbling up the breathless stair
> To burst into fulfilment's desolate attic.

This move requires great tact, since to suggest that his disappointment was more acute than hers would be to indulge in a callous male self-pity: yet the poem tries to suggest something very near to this, while being careful not to dismiss the woman's suffering. It is therefore essential that the poet should admit that he cannot console her, even that he has no right to, but only after a first stanza that so powerfully succeeds in sharing her grief; and equally essential is the line 'For you would hardly care', which admits that her suffering is more important than what the poem then goes on to take as its subject, the deceptions of desire, by means of a metaphor that hovers brilliantly on the edge of a literal account of the story: the attic where the girl was raped turning into 'fulfilment's desolate attic'.

Less deceived: the idea is central to Larkin. In one of his notebooks he wrote, 'Never write anything because you think it's true, only because you think it's beautiful' (Archive); yet he did not act on his own advice. 'Life is first boredom, then fear', runs a line from 'Dockery and Son': Larkin certainly believed this to be true, and it is certainly not beautiful. Indeed, it sounds like an example of how not to write poetry, disastrous in content (who wants poetry that so completely eliminates everything the poets have wanted to write about?), and disastrous in style (a flat sentence, made up of three abstract nouns, one the basic cliché of all versifying, the other two utterly without resonance – 'boredom' is such a boring word). Yet the line has become famous, and it sounds like recognizable Larkin. How did he manage to make poetry out of such statements? To understand this, we must dwell on the contrast which Larkin refers to, that between truth and beauty; but there are other, more illuminating, ways to describe it.

In the famous 'Digression on Madness' in *A Tale of a Tub*, Swift contrasts credulity, which remains satisfied with the outside of things, with curiosity, which 'enters into the depth of things, and comes gravely back with informations and discoveries that in the inside they are good for nothing'; and defines happiness as 'a perpetual possession of being well deceived'. No doubt Larkin had read Swift as a student, but there is no reason to think that this passage was important to him; yet what it says goes to the heart of his poetry. Swift warns us against imagination, which he admits 'can build nobler scenes, and produce more wonderful revolutions, than fortune or nature will ever be able to furnish'. Larkin's poetry offers us the enrichments provided by imagination, and warns us not to be deceived by them: sometimes the poem insists on the enriching, sometimes on the undeceiving. Thus 'Next Please' begins:

> Always too eager for the future, we
> Pick up bad habits of expectancy.
> Something is always approaching; every day
> *Till then* we say.

Cool and admonitory, these lines tell us not to deceive ourselves, not to count on the future bringing us something splendid. The saying that sums up this habit in everyday speech is 'When my ship comes home', and the rest of the poem builds an extended conceit on this:

> Watching from a bluff the tiny, clear
> Armada of promises draw near.
> How slow they are! And how much time they waste,
> Refusing to make haste!

The whole poem is a warning against itself. It develops in loving detail the image of the ships coming towards us, and tells us not to trust them. Credulity delights in the sight of the ship 'leaning with brasswork prinked, | Each rope distinct', and curiosity comes gravely back with the truth:

> Only one ship is seeking us, a black-
> Sailed unfamiliar, towing at her back
> A huge and birdless silence. In her wake
> No waters breed or break.

Yet even this powerful, terrifying conclusion is presented in terms of the very image we were warned against: the ship of death is the one ship that will come home.

The Less Deceived explores this theme, of the deceptions of the imagination, with a richness and variety unsurpassed in post-war English poetry. Sometimes the agent, both of deception and undeception, is language itself:

MAIDEN NAME

> Marrying left your maiden name disused.
> Its five light sounds no longer mean your face,
> Your voice, and all your variants of grace;
> For since you were so thankfully confused
> By law with someone else, you cannot be
> Semantically the same as that young beauty:
> It was of her that these two words were used.
>
> Now it's a phrase applicable to no one,
> Lying just where you left it, scattered through

13

Old lists, old programmes, a school prize or two,
Packets of letters tied with tartan ribbon –
Then is it scentless, weightless, strengthless, wholly
Untruthful? Try whispering it slowly.
No, it means you. Or, since you're past and gone,

It means what we feel now about you then:
How beautiful you were, and near, and young,
So vivid, you must still be there among
Those first few days, unfingermarked again.
So your old name shelters our faithfulness,
Instead of losing shape and meaning less
With your depreciating luggage laden.

This is both a very traditional and a very original poem. There are a thousand poems about how youthful beauty fades: there are hardly any about the fact that women change their names on marrying. We can begin by noticing the word 'semantically': this is both the most and the least important word in the poem. The least important because, as the one unpoetic touch, it functions like a footnote or parenthesis, hardly part of the poem, simply a mention of what kind of remark is being made. And the most important because it tells us that the point of the poem has already been made by language itself. Postmodern poetic theory often claims that the true subject of poetry is language itself, and particularly its unreliability. Larkin's traditional, language-loving poems are a refutation of this theory, yet this poem shows that, paradoxically, they are also a confirmation of it. Although it is a deeply emotional poem about nostalgia, it is also a cool and sophisticated exploration of the meaning of meaning, precise in its logic as it explains how words designate the no-longer-existing past to our present consciousness. The past both does and does not exist: its continued existence takes place in memory and in language. An Elizabethan sonneteer, lamenting the passing of youth and beauty, would remind his beloved of the future 'when winter snows upon your sable hairs', or ask 'Oh how shall summer's honey breath hold out | Against the wrackful siege of battering days?', and in his search for some sort of permanence to youth and beauty would find it in begetting children, or in a Platonic ideal of unchanging love, or in the immortality bestowed by the poem itself. Larkin more modestly finds it only in the fact of language. And his image for the destruction caused by time is similarly low key: instead of the conventional plangent conceits of age snowing white hairs on the beauty, or time as an attacking army, 'digging deep trenches in thy beauty's brow', he ends with 'Instead of losing shape and meaning less | With your depreciating luggage laden' – the gradually increasing shabbiness of one's suitcase (or of all the paraphernalia of one's life seen as 'luggage'). This more casual, more modern choice of image is echoed in the flabbier, more colloquial rhythm and the more slovenly rhyme in the last line: the poem itself begins to depreciate as it turns from the comforting fiction of language to the bleak fact of the passing of time.

Since Larkin's notebooks have been preserved in an archive in the library he ran for thirty years, we can learn a good deal about how he worked on his poems. The versions of 'Maiden Name' show what a meticulous craftsman he was, tinkering with even the smallest detail. The first line began as 'married, you left your maiden name disused', then he changed it to 'Marriage has left...' before settling on 'Marrying left your maiden name disused.' The judgement here is unerring: it is not she but the act of marrying that is responsible for the change; and 'marrying' is better than 'marriage' because it refers to the act rather than the subsequent state. That inspiration may appear not only at the beginning but also at the very end of the process of rewriting is shown by the fact that the brilliant concluding image of the depreciating luggage does not arrive until the final version.

The credulity that, in Swift's words, 'creams off nature, leaving the sour and the dregs for philosophy and reason to lap up' takes many forms: the ship that we tell ourselves is coming home, or the lure of escape. 'Poetry of Departures' is about escaping from the sober responsible life into a dreamed-of bohemianism:

> Sometimes you hear, fifth-hand,
> As epitaph:
> *He chucked up everything*
> *And just cleared off,*
> And always the voice will sound
> Certain you approve
> This audacious, purifying,
> Elemental move.

Typically of Larkin, the poem is not about the man who 'walked out on the whole crowd', but about what the rest of us think about this 'audacious, purifying, | Elemental move'; and it explores this postulated response with great subtlety. Even the title, indulging in an unobtrusive wordplay that one hardly notices at first, appears to be telling us simply that this will be a poem about departures, but turns out to be saying that departure is itself a kind of poetry for the listeners. Once again we are invited to consider whether we trust such poetry, or whether it is simply another deception.

Larkin's most famous treatment of this theme of staying sober and respectable versus chucking everything up is 'Toads':

> Why should I let the toad *work*
>   Squat on my life?
> Can't I use my wit as a pitchfork
>   And drive the brute off?

Asked by an interviewer, 'how did you arrive at the image of a toad for work or labour?', Larkin replied 'sheer genius' (*RW* 74), replacing, for once, mock modesty with mock boasting – and also no doubt showing his reluctance to talk about the process of writing. 'Toads', the funniest poem in the volume, has become one of the best known: it contrasts those who live on their wits ('Lecturers, lispers, | Losels, loblolly-men, louts') with those on whose life the toad *work* continues to squat because 'something sufficiently toad-like' squats in them too. For those who like to read poetry biographically, there are vivid and fascinating links between this poem and the poet's life. Jim Sutton wrote to him in 1950 suggesting that

> a change might do you much good. For instance, physical work, perhaps farming, would surely tend to put to sleep your self-conscious mind? Or you could see the world as a tramp – there are casual wards for tramps where they give you a huge sandwich at night and a huge sandwich in the morning, make you have a bath, and ask no questions. At least I'm told these places still exist today. I'd be most willing to join you in either of these ventures.   (Archive)

Larkin as a farmer!? Larkin as a tramp?! Although Sutton was at that time one of Larkin's closest friends, perhaps the closest, this letter seems almost ludicrous when compared with the sober ordinariness of Larkin's life. For all his youthful contempt for respectability and hard work, he never lived on his wits, hated Bohemianism, and depended on (and valued) the regular routine and respectability he so enjoyed mocking. That is precisely the conclusion of 'Poetry of Departures': that he'd 'go today':

> if
> It weren't so artificial,
> Such a deliberate step backwards
> To create an object:
> Books; china; a life
> Reprehensibly perfect.

Just as the respectable long for escape ('We all hate home'), so those who have escaped would long for respectability and order – so he might as well stay with what, if he chucked it up, would become his object. The tension between the jazz-loving cynic with his coarse language and crude contempt for established values, and the 'death-suited' librarian, correct in behaviour, living in his comfortable flat with its chintzy furniture and fine china, runs all through Larkin's work. Inevitably, the second grew more prominent as he grew older, but poems like 'Toads', 'Toads Revisited', 'Reasons for Attendance', and 'Poetry of Departures' tell us not just that one gives place to the other as youth turns to age, but that they are related symbiotically.

A different tension (which may ultimately be a version of the same one) informs the poem that may well be Larkin's masterpiece, 'Church Going', the longest and most admired poem in *The Less Deceived*. It begins with a comic picture of the poet getting off his bicycle to stop and look round an empty church, bored but impressed, vaguely reverential but conscious of his ignorance as he notices 'some brass and stuff | Up at the holy end', and, as he leaves, wondering why he bothered to stop and look at it: 'Yet stop I did: in fact, I often do.' This introduces a meditation on the future of churches once religion has finally died out: will they turn into museums ('we shall keep | A few cathedrals chronically on show'), or become the haunts of superstition, where 'dubious women come | To make their children touch a particular stone'?. And when finally nothing is left but ruins, who, he wonders, 'will be the last, the very last, to seek | This place for what it was'? Will it be a well-informed expert, a lover of the antiquarian, or a lover of ritual (all described mockingly, in casual diction – 'Some ruin-bibber, randy for antique' or a 'Christmas addict')? Or will he be like the poet, 'Bored, uninformed, knowing the ghostly silt | Dispersed'?

This poem carries further than any other the demythologizing that is so central to Larkin – the deliberate reduction of belief and ritual to social activities with no intrinsic meaning. It springs clearly from the Larkin who declared his dislike of ' "tradition" or a common myth-kitty' as material for poetry. But the demythologizer is always faced with the question, Why do the rituals and beliefs that you are so sure are empty and meaningless mean so much to other people? 'Church Going' confronts this question with honesty and eloquence as it moves to its marvellous close:

> For though I've no idea
> What this accoutred frowsty barn is worth,
> It pleases me to stand in silence here;
>
> A serious house on serious earth it is,
> In whose blent air all our compulsions meet,
> Are recognised, and robed as destinies.
> And that much never can be obsolete,
> Since someone will forever be surprising
> A hunger in himself to be more serious...

A crucial word in this passage is 'serious', which in the last century possessed the meaning 'religious'. Not only does this meaning fit the poem beautifully, it calls attention to the fact that a word which primarily describes a human state of mind has shifted to having a religious meaning, so suggesting that religion is human in its origins. After demythologizing comes remythologizing: not the claim that the beliefs were true after all, but an understanding of what has led people to devise them. The 'compulsions' are not compulsions to believe in God: people have believed in God as a way of organizing their secular and human compulsions. First comes the 'hunger', the need for reverence; then we build a barn to satisfy it, and construct beliefs to authorize the accoutrements. That need will remain after the very last person has sought the church out 'for what it was'. No Christian can take much comfort from this view, or from the assurance that our compulsions 'are recognised and robed as destinies', for it tells us that our beautiful beliefs are fictions. Hence the conclusion:

18

> And gravitating with it to this ground,
> Which, he once heard, was proper to grow wise in,
> If only that so many dead lie round.

'He once heard': this means, heard about how people constructed beliefs for themselves because they needed them. They accoutred the barn, and there must have been a point to it. When we are serious, we see the point, but the seriousness is something wholly secular, even pagan.

Once again, a look a Larkin's notebook tells us a lot about how this poem grew. Originally, it began very differently: 'Into them, into their weekday silence', 'I am drawn into their weekday silence', 'How strange, these numerous unaltered buildings', 'Why am I brought repeatedly up and down', 'What brings me time and again into your silences | Up and down England' (Archive): these very different versions of the opening all differ strikingly from the poem we have, since they start not with an anecdote but with the reflections that Larkin finally decided to leave for the third stanza. Only then, with the line 'Yet stop I did: in fact I often do', does he move from the anecdote to his general reflections. 'Often' in this line corresponds to 'repeatedly' or 'time and again' in the earlier openings (at one stage he even seems to have thought of making 'repeatedly' the opening word), and by saving this touch till later he gives the poem the vivid narrative opening that has appealed to so many readers (though it should be added that putting the anecdote in the simple present tense, which is normally used in English for habitual or repeated acts, prepares us unobtrusively for the generalization 'in fact I often do').

Of the many other things we can learn from the notebook drafts about the fashioning of this poem, one point in particular seems especially worth mention. Larkin clearly thought carefully about how explicit the Christian references should be. In a poem about the doubtful survival of a religious institution, there must be a case both for and against using religious language. At one stage the poet wrote:

> Upon this ground
> So many lives lie thick, so many deaths
> And births and marriages; so many said
> *Lord have mercy upon us* here, or knew
> At last how vain things are.

> (Archive)

'Lord have mercy upon us' is, of course, what many of the churchgoers would have said. Knowing 'at last how vain things are' is also what they might have thought, since Christianity, in its more puritanical forms at least, teaches the vanity of all earthly things – though the words here are much more likely to mean that their prayers and their hope of resurrection were vain. Both these lines were in the end rejected, removing still further any invitation to the reader to accept the church on its own terms. Its ongoing importance must rest only on being the site for rites of passage.

4

The Whitsun Weddings

Since Philip Larkin never married, and never owned a house until he was over 50, he spent most of his adult life in rented accommodation. This began in Wellington, where his first lodgings were small, chilly, and lacking in privacy; as he grew more prosperous his lodgings naturally became more spacious, culminating in the comfortable flat in Pearson Park where he lived for eighteen years; but he never lost the feeling of rootlessness, and out of it came one of his bleakest and most powerful poems, 'Mr Bleaney':

> 'This was Mr Bleaney's room. He stayed
> The whole time he was at the Bodies, till
> They moved him.' Flowered curtains, thin and frayed,
> Fall to within five inches of the sill,
>
> Whose window shows a strip of building land,
> Tussocky, littered....

The clinical, appraising glance that registers the expected drawbacks ('Bed, upright chair, sixty-watt bulb, no hook | Behind the door, no room for books or bags') shows us that the speaker is all too familiar with life in hired rooms, and the moment of decision ('I'll take it') is not heroic but a tired acceptance of the inevitable. 'So it happens that I lie | Where Mr Bleaney lay'; and the rest of the poem sets forth the poet's feelings of frustration by means of a speculation about the predecessor he never met. 'I know his habits', he tells us, learnt obviously from the talkative landlady; then he lists these habits in all their emptiness, and concludes:

> But if he stood and watched the frigid wind
> Tousling the clouds, lay on the fusty bed
> Telling himself that this was home, and grinned,
> And shivered without shaking off the dread

> That how we live measures our own nature,
> And at his age having no more to show
> Than one hired box should make him pretty sure
> He warranted no better, I don't know.

This is a masterly use of syntax. Do these frightening thoughts belong to Mr Bleaney, or to the poet? The externals of a person's life are available to observation, the feelings are known only to himself; so we would naturally assume this chilling account of futility to be an account of how the poet himself feels – except that he is careful not to say so. The use of Mr Bleaney as the subject of the poem is a brilliant device for avoiding self-pity. If how we live measures our own nature, it might measure the poet's too, but we are left to draw that conclusion for ourselves.

'Mr Bleaney' is the second poem in *The Whitsun Weddings*, and perhaps the most brilliant. When an interviewer remarked to Larkin that his favourite subjects were failure and weakness he objected: 'A good poem about failure is a success' (*RW* 74). Mr Bleaney could not have written 'Mr Bleaney'.

The Whitsun Weddings is full of small masterpieces – 'Love Songs in Age', 'Dockery and Son', and the title poem, which dominates the volume as 'Church Going' dominated *The Less Deceived*. 'The Whitsun Weddings' is an account of a train journey from Hull to London. The description has all Larkin's brilliantly succinct observation ('A hothouse flashed uniquely: hedges dipped | And rose'), and this slowly gives place to an awareness that honeymoon couples are getting on the train at every station, couples who will never meet, but whose lives 'would all contain this hour'.

> fathers had never known
> Success so huge and wholly farcical;
>   The women shared
> The secret like a happy funeral;
> While girls, gripping their handbags tighter, stared
> At a religious wounding....

The vivid, accurate description of the wedding parties is poised between seeing them as ordinary, even ridiculous, and passing on the intensity of the participants. The religious wounding is both the ceremony and the ensuing night, the girls are staring both at what is in front of them and at what they are imagining.

Just as the unbeliever, thinking about religion in 'Church Going', is led to ask himself what all the fuss is about, so the bachelor watches the weddings in this poem, finds them comic and, to the fastidious eye, in poor taste ('The nylon gloves and jewellery-substitutes'), but struggles to express the mysterious importance of the 'frail | Travelling coincidence'.

This poem makes it clearer than any other that Larkin was the laureate of modern Britain, the precise observer of daily life and class distinctions, the recorder of the ordinary, reaching beyond observation, often to boredom and anomie, but also to mysterious richness. The sacred, according to Durkheim, is essentially a social concept, to which supernatural beliefs are added as a kind of extra; and in that sense Larkin the atheist is, at his finest, a poet of the sacred.

Larkin's subjects range from the most conventional to the most unpoetic; so let us juxtapose two poems from *The Whitsun Weddings* to see how great the contrast is. A woman sings love-songs, and grows old; an advertisement hoarding looms over a slum – the first the subject of a hundred poems, the second of none. The first is private, sentimental, touching; the second public, brassy, commercial. Both the love-songs and the advertisements are attempts to make life less boring, less frightening: all such attempts are lies. Lies that are believed in become myths, so the difference between 'Love Songs in Age' and 'Essential Beauty' may not be as great as the obvious difference between the subjects. The first deals with a conventionally poetic subject, and deploys enormous skill to retain conventionally poetic beauties. It looks and feels as one expects a poem about love to look and feel, then culminates in the calm assertion that the love-songs were all lies, an assertion placed prominently and explicitly at the end, destroying the point of the poem and leaving it unharmed.

Advertisements, on the other hand, as we all know, are full of lies, but if you believe them then they too become myths. So 'Essential Beauty', which is a poem about advertisements on hoardings, does not need to remind us of their trickery; it can devote all its eloquence to their beauty:

> they rise
> Serenely to proclaim pure crust, pure foam,
> Pure coldness to our live imperfect eyes

> That stare beyond this world, where nothing's made
> As new or washed quite clean, seeking the home
> All such inhabit....

The most famous myth about a possible world where everything attains the perfection never found in this life is Plato's doctrine of the Forms. The very expression 'essential beauty' suggests Plato, who wrote: 'What may we suppose to be the felicity of the man who sees absolute beauty in its essence, pure and unalloyed, who instead of a beauty tainted by human flesh and colour and a mass of perishable rubbish, is able to apprehend divine beauty where it exists apart and alone.' The absolute beauty of Plato's *Symposium* would not be much like pure crust and pure foam, since it has no appeal to the senses; but the advertisement too floats us up into a realm where we do not actually taste and feel the idealized product. The suggestion that an advertisement hoarding gives access to the Platonic essence of beauty is absurd and magnificent. There is no need for this poem to end like 'Love Songs in Age', with a sobering statement that the transforming power of love does not transform, for we have known that all along. Instead it ends with an image of almost unfathomable ambivalence:

> dying smokers sense
> Walking towards them through some dappled park
> As if on water that unfocused she
> No match lit up, nor drag ever brought near,
> Who now stands newly clear,
> Smiling, and recognising, and going dark.

Smoking, as the government warning reminds us, is bad for your health; but then you die anyway. Platonic beauty is a lie, advertiser's patter is a lie; but without such lies, life would be merely boredom and fear. Death, as the poets have often told us, is the mother of beauty. This is Larkin's way of saying it.

5

High Windows – and Larkin's Politics

Since his death, Larkin has been attacked by some critics for his reactionary opinions and misogynistic attitudes. Lisa Jardine, for instance, describes him as 'a casual habitual racist, and an easy misogynist. Not to mention a malicious gossip, who relished savagely caricaturing fellow authors and critics, and abusing acquaintances.' She describes the cultural frame within which Larkin writes as one which 'takes racism and sexism for granted as crucially a part of the British national heritage'. Peter Ackroyd (writing of Larkin in a way that strikingly recalls Larkin's own words about his mother) refers to 'that drab monologue of misery and self-pity which was to fill his letters and poems', claims that he was essentially a minor poet 'who for purely local and temporary reasons acquired a large reputation', and asserts that 'by the end of his life he had become a foul-mouthed bigot'. Not many of the attacks on Larkin's reactionary views are as virulent as these (though one correspondent in the *Library Association Record* did suggest that he should be banned!); but a popular view has grown up, often among those who have read little or none of his work, that it is vitiated by hatred, spite, and envy. To ask if there is any truth in this view can provide a starting-point for discussing some of the poems in *High Windows*.

'I've always been right-wing,' said Larkin in an interview. 'It's difficult to say why, but not being a political thinker, I suppose I identify the Right with certain virtues (thrift, hard work, reverence, desire to preserve) and the Left with certain vices' (*RW* 52). This is here expressed with the restraint appropriate to a public statement, but in his letters he is often fiercer. 'My simple cure for "unemployment" (no such thing really) is to abolish unemployment benefits. If you don't want chaps to do a thing, then don't pay them to do it.' Or – even fiercer, even hysterical – 'I find the "state of the nation" quite terrifying. In ten years time we shall *all* be cowering under our beds as rampaging hordes of blacks steal anything they can lay hands on' (*SL* 646, 755).

How far must these views influence, or even undermine, our appreciation of Larkin's poetry? For those who share his political views, there will presumably be no problem: his considered declaration of conservative sympathies, and his high opinion of Mrs Thatcher, would appeal to large numbers of the British, including many thoughtful people, and even the more outrageous statements he made in letters are widely shared – though not perhaps by many readers of poetry. But the very outrageousness of his racist statements might also be seen as a reason for not taking them too seriously. Few of us would feel comfortable if every unkind remark and casual prejudice were quoted as evidence of our deep-seated corruption; Larkin himself remarked 'My political opinions are really no more than gouts of bile' (*SL* 650).

There are a few crude right-wing poems by Larkin, all short and most of them unpublished. These I believe can be pushed aside as trivia which are best forgotten; one comparatively crude poem which he did publish ('Homage to a Government') stands out for the unsubtle quality of its irony, and has few admirers. More interesting is the question whether Larkin's best work is in any way touched by political views that many find controversial and even unacceptable.

'Thrift, hard work, reverence, desire to preserve': not, for everybody, the most important social virtues, but virtues none the less. Are they central to Larkin's poetry? Two of the longer poems in *High Windows* could be described as celebrations of tradition. In both cases, it is a tradition of the ordinary rather than of pomp and circumstance. 'To the Sea' describes an afternoon at the seaside, with family outings that remind the poet of his own childhood, 'Still going on, all of it, still going on!' 'Show Saturday' describes an agricultural show in great detail listing almost everything that is to be seen there in deliberately pedestrian fashion ('a beer-marquee that | Half-screens a canvas Gents; a tent selling tweed, | And another, jackets'), and then relating how it is all packed up and everyone returns to 'private addresses'. Both poems are matter of fact in their descriptive style, making no attempt to romanticize or render the everyday scene unfamiliar; both convey affection for and approval of the activity they so carefully describe. Both could be seen as expressions of 'reverence and a desire to preserve': indeed, 'Show Saturday' concludes 'Let it be always there'. A thoughtful conservative reader might indeed feel that these poems spring from conservative sympathies, that both are about the way work and leisure sustain each other. Such a reader might murmur approvingly, as the show is packed away,

> Let it stay hidden there like strength, below
> Sale-bills and swindling; something people do,
> Not noticing how time's rolling smithy-smoke
> Shadows much greater gestures.

It is certainly possible to read the poems this way, but that would be to use the term 'conservative' in a very wide sense. The poems do indeed celebrate ordinariness, and do see it is a kind of tradition, but whether the celebration of ordinariness belongs more to the Left or the Right in politics is not easy to say. If ordinariness is contrasted with pomp and ceremony and military bravura, it is likely to appeal to the Left; if contrasted with unorthodoxy and a passion to change things, it will appeal to the Right. Radicals are on the whole opposed to tradition only when it is used to uphold the existing power relations in society. It is true that the British Conservative Party harnessed the idea of family values to its programme in the 1980s, and 'To the Sea' concludes with praise of family values:

> It may be that through habit these do best,
> Coming to water clumsily undressed
> Yearly; teaching their children by a sort
> Of clowning; helping the old, too, as they ought.

This has come a long way from the youthful cynicism of the Larkin who declared that people were not designed to live together, that family life was a kind of Hell! The now elderly Larkin has put only the positive element of his right-wing sympathies into this poem, none of the hostility and dislike of foreigners and blacks. There is no reason, either, to attribute any of these prejudices to the respectable families helping the old, as

they ought, who are undressing clumsily on the beach. Its praise
of ordinariness is virtually unpolitical.

But: there is always a but. Are the carefully written and
judicious utterances of a poet more important, and more central
to his poetry, than his 'gouts of bile'? To answer this, let us turn
to one of his most disturbing poems, 'The Old Fools'.

> What do they think has happened, the old fools,
> To make them like this? Do they somehow suppose
> It's more grown-up when your mouth hangs open and drools,
> And you keep on pissing yourself, and can't remember
> Who called this morning?
>
> .   .   .   .   .
> Why aren't they screaming?

How should we react to the old, especially those who have
entered senility? Convention and human decency both require
us to treat them with respect, to attend to what is positive, to
remember that they are still persons; the speaker of 'To the Sea'
would want us do this, 'as we ought'. But 'The Old Fools' flies in
the face of convention and decency: not only does it linger on
everything that is most disgusting about old age, it abuses the
old, tells us that it is *their fault* that they are mindless and
incontinent. It is a deeply offensive poem, the product not of the
sober dark-suited librarian but of the disrespectful, foul-
mouthed undergraduate.

To condemn a poet for being a 'foul-mouthed bigot' or a
'malicious gossip', to point out that he was mean with money or
treated his womenfolk badly, is a dangerous form of argument
for a literary critic. Not, of course, because bigotry, malice, and
selfishness should be defended, but for two closely related
reasons. In the first place, this is condemnation of the man and
of his opinions, not of his work: and, though the sort of criticism
which looks at the personal or political context of poetry is
legitimate and even illuminating, this context must be invoked
in order to ask what light it throws on the poetry, not to run the
two together as if it and the surrounding opinions were the
same thing, and had the same kind of importance, as poems.
And secondly, and more important, for a reason well stated by
the Irish dramatist J. M. Synge in his Preface to his *Poems and
Translations* of 1908: 'it is the timber of poetry that wears best,
and there is no timber that has not strong roots among the clay

and worms.' Solemn public statements, careful not to offend, are a long way from poetry; and 'To the Sea' has, perhaps, too much of the public statement about it. Splenetic outbursts may tap a source much closer to inspiration; and that is why wanting 'The Old Fools' toned down to compassion and respectability is to be blind to its power. It is a howl of rage at senility, and behind the rage lies fear. Logic no doubt requires that the rage be directed at the passage of time and at Alzheimer's disease, but we do not feel rage at such abstractions, we feel rage at people, and in this case the people are the disgusting, drooling old. A helpful parallel is offered in a poem by Larkin's favourite poet:

> Why did you give no hint that night
> That quickly after the morrow's dawn,
> And calmly, as if indifferent quite,
> You would close your term here, up and be gone...
>
> Never to bid goodbye,
> Or lip me the softest call...

When someone close to us dies we feel betrayed and angry, and the closer we are to the person the more likely we are to blame her. We do not feel that way if we look at the death with uninvolved regret; it is betrayed love (how could you do this to me?) that is moved to anger. That is why Thomas Hardy, writing a poem to his dead wife, *rebukes* her for leaving him. The title of the poem, 'The Going', is deliberately ambiguous: she not only died, she left him. Of course Hardy does not abuse her with the coarseness that Larkin directs at the old men: this may derive from when the poems were written. In 1912 a poem was thought of as an utterance that needed to preserve the decencies; in 1973 such restraint has gone.

If Larkin's poem continued in the same abusive vein it would be powerful and nasty, with a nastiness that gives us a moral shock. But in the next stanzas it sees old age from within – or tries to (the third stanza begins 'Perhaps') – through a haunting image of 'having lighted rooms Inside your head', rooms with

> a fire burning,
> The blown bush at the window, or the sun's
> Faint friendliness on the wall some lonely
> Rain-ceased midsummer evening....

Then the poem reverts from this glimpse of lost happiness to the bleakness of age, and once again they are called 'the old fools', 'crouching below | Extinction's alp...never perceiving| How near it is'. The anger now is calmer, less frenetic, even more painful, as the poem ends with a grim reminder that our turn will come.

To wish away the offensive coarseness of this poem would be an insensitive, sentimentalizing reading.

Coarseness is a striking feature of Larkin's later poems. His letters to his male friends had always been coarse, and in his final volume he allowed the coarseness into his poems. This has become, not surprisingly, the best-known feature of his work, but to appreciate what it is for we must remember two things. First, that almost all the poems of Larkin's maturity are in regular metre with rhyme: the violently disruptive shift of register takes place within a meticulous avoidance of formal disruption. And, secondly, the poems that begin with coarseness usually go on to end in transfiguring beauty. The most striking example of this is the title poem of the volume:

HIGH WINDOWS

When I see a couple of kids
And guess he's fucking her and she's
Taking pills or wearing a diaphragm,
I know this is paradise

Everyone old has dreamed of all their lives –
Bonds and gestures pushed to one side
Like an outdated combine harvester,
And everyone young going down the long slide

To happiness, endlessly. I wonder if
Anyone looked at me, forty years back,
And thought, *That'll be the life*;
No God any more, or sweating in the dark

About hell and that, or having to hide
What you think of the priest. He
And his lot will all go down the long slide
Like free bloody birds. And immediately

Rather than words comes the thought of high windows:
The sun-comprehending glass,
And beyond it, the deep blue air, that shows
Nothing, and is nowhere, and is endless.

The movement of this poem is in two steps. The first stanza is obviously meant to shock: not only will the coarse, explicit language offend some readers; there is another, and less obvious, offensiveness in its assumption that sex is for men and contraceptive precautions are for women. Then this sour coarse envy is pushed aside, first, by the theme of the cycle of generations: I am old and envious of sexual freedom, and in my time I represented freedom from religion – was that too envied by the old? Both these emancipations are represented by the same image, that of 'the long slide', which at one time Larkin considered as a possible title for the poem. And it is not difficult to see why: it is an image that can suggest either exhilaration or panic, the delight of moving freely down, or the fear of being out of control. The panic is only the faintest of hints in the first use, but the second time the image is more disquieting, with its suggestion that 'he and his lot' are contemptible as well as lucky.

And then, finally, the theme of new, liberated generations is pushed aside, not by another step in the argument, but by an image that opens onto nothing. It is not the first image in the poem, but, whereas the logical function of the combine harvester can be stated with complete accuracy, and that of the long slide with a high degree of approximation, the final image is utterly open-ended. It is interesting, no doubt, to discover that Larkin liked living in top-floor flats, that when he bought a house, late in life, he wrote 'I hate living on the ground floor; all my poems were written on top floors' (*SL* 623), but though that makes it clear that the image held great power for him, it does not tell us what its function in the poem is. Is it a figure for happiness, the happiness he was supposed to have had and the kids are supposed (by him) to be having – and if it is, does it tell us that happiness is as liberating as the deep blue air and the comprehending of the sun, or as empty as the last line? Or is it a figure for the comparison itself – that to see in these kids his own forty-years-ago self is to look through the high windows into bliss – or into nothingness? In other words, it can be an image contributed by the persona who speaks the poem, or by the scriptor who writes it; and in each case, it is ambiguous.

Larkin is a poet of absence. His roads have fallen into disuse, many of his characteristic epithets ('unpriceable', 'unfathomable', 'unfingermarked') state negatives, and one of his own favourite lines sees the beauty of seascapes, and loves it because it suggests 'Such attics cleared of me! Such absences!' It is not surprising, therefore, that 'High Windows' ends with a glimpse into absence and emptiness.

The Less Deceived and *The Whitsun Weddings* are both dominated by a poem longer than the others, which offers a complex exploration of issues central both to the poet and to our society, and which has become the most famous poem in the volume. No single poem dominates *High Windows* in quite the same way, but the nearest candidate is probably 'The Building': certainly this has much in common with 'Church Going', also a poem about a building which moves from looking at it to reflecting on its function, and its relationship with death.

> Higher than the handsomest hotel
> The lucent comb shows up for miles, but see,
> All round it close-ribbed streets rise and fall
> Like a great sigh out of the last century.
> The porters are scruffy; what keep drawing up
> At the entrance are not taxis; and in the hall
> As well as creepers hangs a frightening smell.

What is this 'lucent comb'? Twenty years earlier Larkin had written a poem called 'Hospital Visits' (which he never published), a mildly ironic, Hardyesque anecdote about a woman who broke her wrist when visiting her dying husband in hospital. To compare these two poems is to see something of how the mature Larkin developed. Though it is soon obvious that 'The Building' is about a hospital, we are never told this, a silence that is somehow mysteriously eloquent. It corresponds perhaps to the evasiveness we associate with illness, our unwillingness to utter words like 'death' or 'cancer'; but it also invites us to make it strange, to look at the building as if we did not know what such places are for. Hence the almost quaint way in which this first stanza seems to be trying to work out whether it is a hotel or not.

Two ideas run through the poem. One is the contrast between the hospital and the world outside:

> Traffic, a locked church; short terraced streets
> Where kids chalk games, and girls with hair-dos fetch

> Their separates from the cleaners – O world,
> Your loves, your chances, are beyond the stretch
> Of any hand from here!...

That world is ordinary, even drab – but alive, and suddenly attractive when seen from inside the building. The other idea is more elusive, but strangely powerful: it explores this building as the modern attempt to build a defence against dying. From the beginning, the poem invites us to ask, What is the building for, and the thought becomes explicit at the end:

> That is what it means,
> This clean-sliced cliff; a struggle to transcend
> The thought of dying, for unless its powers
> Outbuild cathedrals nothing contravenes
> The coming dark, though crowds each evening try
>
> With wasteful, weak, propitiatory flowers.

Of course nothing *can* contravene the coming dark. The building may, in the literal sense, 'outbuild cathedrals' – it is taller – but its 'powers' are no greater than the now outmoded religion. We cannot overcome death, but we keep refusing to accept it. Hence the moving ending, which places such weight on the word 'try', and concludes with the brilliant image of the flowers. The visitors bring flowers, of course, for their friends and relatives who are ill, but if you step back and look at the functioning of the whole building, it looks as if they are brought as offerings on the altar of death – a helpless, futile act of propitiation.

6

The Larkin Persona

We have already seen that Larkin's poems often draw on the poet's own experiences, and biographical readings, which attract so many readers, can sometimes be illuminating; but we have also seen that they need to be made with care. This is such an important issue for Larkin's poetry, and raises such an important question in literary criticism, that it is now necessary to turn to a discussion of Larkin's use of a persona – a device that runs right through his work, and is often crucial to understanding the relationship between man and poem.

It was a commonplace of Romantic poetic theory that poetry, especially lyric poetry, is the most direct of human utterances, the unmediated, unevasive expression of the poet's emotion. Keats strove to capture 'the true voice of feeling' in his poems, Wordsworth defined poetry as 'the spontaneous overflow of powerful feelings', and praised Shakespeare's sonnets because in them the poet 'unlocked his heart'; Ruskin defined lyric poetry as 'the expression by the poet of his own feelings'. The reaction against this view in the twentieth century claimed that the poetic speaker is always constructed, that even the most apparently personal lyric has a dramatic speaker distinct from the poet; and as a result it has become common to refer to the 'I' of a poem not as 'Shelley' or 'Yeats' or 'Larkin', but as 'the speaker' or 'the persona'.

Of course nineteenth-century critics knew perfectly well that not all poetry was directly uttered by the poet. We cannot identify every character in *Macbeth* or *Othello* with Shakespeare, since it is the very nature of drama that it depicts interaction between different persons, so that when we read a speech by Othello or Iago we attend not only to what is said, but also to who is saying it. A Romantic theorist will no doubt claim that

Macbeth's despair ('Life's but a walking shadow...a tale | Told by an idiot') springs from some deep experience of the author's, but he still knows that the experience of reading Macbeth's speeches is not the same as that of reading a despairing sonnet (like No. 66) of Shakespeare's, since we are constantly aware that we are listening not to a self-contained expression of emotion but to Macbeth, the man whose story is unfolding before us.

There is, in other words, a difference between lyric and dramatic poetry; and, whereas the Romantics insisted on the lyric element in dramatic poetry, the modern tendency is rather to find a dramatic element in the lyric: to claim that, although the 'I' of a lyric poem is not an invented speaker, he should not be identified with the person who wrote the poem. The best way to formulate this point is to use the concept of *persona*. Originally, the Latin *persona* meant a mask; then, because the actors in Greek drama wore masks, it meant a character in a play (we still refer to the list of characters as 'dramatis personae'); then, in twentieth-century criticism, it has come to mean a version of the author, a mask worn by the poet, a way in which he conveys to the reader 'this is and is not me'. Its most useful meaning as a critical term equates it neither with the poet himself, on the one hand, nor with a fictitious speaker, on the other (we already have terms for both these concepts), but refers to the conscious playing by the poet of a role that bears a close relation to the self.

All this is of central importance for a discussion of Larkin. Look, for instance, at:

A STUDY OF READING HABITS

When getting my nose in a book
Cured most things short of school,
It was worth ruining my eyes
To know I could still keep cool,
And deal out the old right hook
To dirty dogs twice my size.

Later, with inch-thick specs,
Evil was just my lark:
Me and my cloak and fangs
Had ripping times in the dark.
The women I clubbed with sex!
I broke them up like meringues.

Don't read much now: the dude
Who lets the girl down before
The hero arrives, the chap
Who's yellow and keeps the store,
Seem far too familiar. Get stewed:
Books are a load of crap.

It is easy to find in Larkin's letters and in his friends' reminiscences a strong strain of dismissive remarks on literature. As an undergraduate he wrote in the college library copy of Spenser: 'First I thought Troilus and Criseyde was the most boring poem in English. Then I thought Beowulf was. Then I thought Paradise Lost was. Now I *know* that the Faerie Queen is the *dullest thing out. Blast it.' (Life, 59).* It is understandable, then, that some readers have identified the speaker of this poem with its author, although the title asks us quite explicitly not to do this. The whole point of the poem is that it is about a particular kind of reading, reading for direct wish-fulfilment. According to one of Freud's more simplistic theories, this is the basis of all literary pleasure, and Larkin here offers us a crude example of this, the reader who is inadequate in life because he is bullied and unattractive, and consoles himself in fantasy by winning fights and taking sadistic pleasure in sex when he reads; then we are told that this pleasure will let us down as the reader comes to realize that he is actually more like the unattractive figures than the hero. Read in the crude Freudian way, and you will end up concluding that 'books are a load of crap'.

In contrast, let us turn now to 'Aubade'.

I work all day, and get half-drunk at night.
Waking at four to soundless dark, I stare.
In time the curtain-edges will grow light.
Till then I see what's really always there:
Unresting death, a whole day nearer now,
Making all thought impossible but how
And where and when I shall myself die.
Arid interrogation: yet the dread
Of dying, and being dead,
Flashes afresh to hold and horrify.

The mind blanks at the glare. Not in remorse
– The good not done, the love not given, time
Torn off unused – nor wretchedly because
An only life can take so long to climb

Clear of its wrong beginnings, and may never;
But at the total emptiness for ever,
The sure extinction that we travel to
And shall be lost in always. Not to be here,
Not to be anywhere,
And soon; nothing more terrible, nothing more true.

Once again, we can match the poem against direct utterances by the poet. 'I think it's amazing', he wrote, 'the way people don't seem to worry about death. Of course one ought to be brave and all that, but it's never been anything but a terrible source of dread to me' (*SL* 576). To a sociologist he wrote 'it's hard to say whether fear of death is a neurotic condition... My first impulse is to say that it is simply seeing things clearly' (*SL* 591). This time the match is close and – surely – more important. The tremendous power of 'Aubade' – the last major poem Larkin wrote – springs from the conviction that every word is meant, that we are watching someone who is not performing a part but expressing his deepest feelings. The effect of the poem would be weakened if it was offered as a 'study' of the fear of death, inviting us not to share the terror but to observe the way such a person thinks and talks. The sophisticated reader who feels only ironic detachment from the speaker will appreciate 'A Study of Reading Habits' to the full, but will be almost incapacitated from responding to the power of 'Aubade'.

Poetic theories are inadequate if they assume that all poems are the same. Theories that apply equally to all poems may be useful for some purposes, but for the reading of actual poems we need to be aware of the particularities of each. It is, therefore, necessary for us to realize that the claim that every poem has a dramatic speaker distinct from the author cannot be indiscriminately applied, or it will blur the crucial distinction between these two poems.

But even this stark contrast must not be made too stark. No utterance can be completely spontaneous, since in order to communicate with its hearers it must make use of conventions that the hearer will understand, and these conventions will leave their mark on what is said. 'Aubade' is suffused with awareness that it is a poem: not only because of the immaculate metre and careful rhyme scheme, but also because of the title. *Aubade* means 'dawn song', and the *aubade* or *alba* was a well-known and popular lyric genre in the Middle Ages, in which the lover bids farewell to his beloved, since the coming of day means that he must leave her. Larkin's poem makes no explicit reference to this tradition, but the title invites us to notice the contrast: this speaker is not with his beloved but alone, he grieves when dawn comes not because the joys of love and companionship are over but because he is terrified of death. The great unspoken absence in this poem is the beloved.

It is even possible that there is a more explicit reference. One of the great modern poems about old age is T. S. Eliot's 'Little Gidding', in which the poet meets a ghost of all his literary ancestors the morning after an air raid, and is forced to confront 'the gifts reserved for age', which include

> the shame
> Of motives late revealed, and the awareness
> Of things ill done, and done to others' harm
> Which once you took for exercise of virtue.

Larkin's denial that his pain is caused by remorse for 'the good not done, the love not given' (that sounds like a line from 'Little Gidding') may be an explicit rejection of the dawn thoughts of Eliot – a literary allusion for the well-read to pick up.

Now we must insert a further complication. I have so far assumed as unproblematic the idea of a direct utterance with which we can contrast the complexities of speaking through a persona. But how do we find examples of such directness? In looking at the poet's letters or reported remarks, we cannot ignore the possibility that they too are refracted through conventions and may be spoken through a persona. The letters to Robert Conquest (literary friend who shared both Larkin's taste for pornography and his right-wing opinions), to Monica Jones (lifelong intimate companion), and to Anthony Thwaite and Douglas Dunn (younger poets whom he respected and liked) are quite different from one another in tone. In one letter to Thwaite he refers rather uneasily to a forthcoming 'personal appearance': 'The awful thing is that people may be expecting too much – a combination of Rupert Brooke, Walt Whitman and T. S. Eliot, instead of which they get bald deaf bicycle-clipped Larkin, the Laforgue of Pearson Park' (SL 460). This ironic account of the presentation of self in everyday life makes it clear that direct encounter with other people can be a contrived situation, mediated by role-playing.

A letter of 1975 to his college friend Norman Iles says: 'Had a letter from a girl in Ramsgate saying how disgusting my poems were – "sick and lustful". Whoops. The only ones she cited were *very* mild. Thank God she's in Ramsgate' (*SL* 524). The self-awareness embodied in this is complex and subtle. 'Whoops' is presumably an exclamation of warning (watch it – you'll get into trouble) but surely expresses delight as well. He is enjoying the experience of pretending to be alarmed at what might happen to him from disapproving readers, amused at the thought that he could show the girl far worse poems, and at the same time aware that the girl is exposing her naïvety in taking the poems as biographical documents depicting his sick lust (yet he is prepared to admit that he is sick and lustful too).

It is, in short, another example of self-presentation. Have we no knowledge, then, of Larkin as he 'really was' – nothing but a series of personae? The fact that we cannot have unmediated access to the consciousness of others has led some sociologists and literary theorists to deny that we can know anything except the process of mediation, that, locked in a prison house of language, we have no direct access to non-linguistic reality. This would mean that everything we speak or write is conveyed through a persona, that there is no such thing as simply telling the truth about ourselves. But we all know from our own consciousness that there *is* such a thing as experience, and that what we say about it can be more or less sincere, more or less genuine. From the fact of our own experience lying behind what we say, we deduce that others too feel love, hate, fear, loneliness, and joy, that what they say derives from experience and can be more or less misleading about it. The fact that we can have no direct access to the experience of others does not mean that we must deny its existence.

Like everyone else, Larkin presented himself in everyday life through a series of personae, some more consciously assumed and more misleading than others; the deliberate use of a persona is central to some of his poems and to some of his statements, is less noticeable in others, and is sometimes as absent as is possible in poetry. I chose 'A Study of Reading Habits' and 'Aubade' as representing the two extremes; now in conclusion I return to 'Church Going' to look more closely at the opening stanzas.

> Once I am sure there's nothing going on
> I step inside, letting the door thud shut.
> Another church: matting, seats, and stone,
> And little books; sprawlings of flowers, cut
> For Sunday, brownish now; some brass and stuff
> Up at the holy end; the small neat organ;
> And a tense, musty, unignorable silence,
> Brewed God knows how long. Hatless, I take off
> My cycle-clips in awkward reverence,
>
> Move forward, run my hand around the font.
> From where I stand, the roof looks almost new –
> Cleaned, or restored? Someone would know: I don't.
> Mounting the lectern, I peruse a few
> Hectoring large-scale verses, and pronounce
> 'Here endeth' much more loudly than I'd meant.
> The echoes snigger briefly. Back at the door
> I sign the book, donate an Irish sixpence,
> Reflect the place was not worth stopping for.

Larkin informed John Betjeman in an interview that he was fond of visiting churches, and this self-portrait contains a good deal of factual accuracy, even down to its trivial details: he often visited churches by bicycle, he was living in Belfast when he wrote the poem so is likely to have had Irish money in his pocket. Yet none of the details is there merely because it is factually correct: they build the picture of the awkward amateur wondering if he really wants to be there, the vague and uninformed reverence of the modern unbeliever. He gives sixpence but it is not a real gift because it's the wrong currency: the detail fits the situation perfectly, and there is no need to claim that the church is in Ireland (indeed, to do so would weaken the effect). He pretends for a moment to be reading the lesson, but his feeling that he is an intruder is stronger than his enjoyment of the role, so that he only succeeds in making himself feel embarrassed, and hearing a 'snigger' in the echoes is, once again, a detail that captures this perfectly: the brief mockery of a church service turns into a mockery of himself. This is exactly what is meant by persona: choosing from one's actual behaviour details that draw amused attention to the kind of person he is. Larkin is acting the role of being Larkin.

7

Larkin and Literary Criticism

Larkin collected his critical essays in the volume called *Required Writing*, which appeared in 1983. For the reader of his poetry it is a fascinating book, offering a highly personal view of contemporary literature which tells us a good deal about his preferences and prejudices, as well as containing some splendid insights into the writers themselves. From his review of Iona and Peter Opie's *Lore and Language of Schoolchildren* in 1960 we learn about the moment of revelation when he realized 'that it was not people I disliked but children', and are told that for the simple fact that children are in the process of turning into adults 'they may be forgiven much'. From his review of *Homage to Clio* (also 1960) we learn that, in Larkin's view, Auden changed around 1940 into a quite different and greatly inferior poet: only in the early Auden does he find the 'dominant and ubiquitous unease' that quickened his sensibilities and produced a truly modern poetry that embodied 'not only the age's properties but its obsessions'. In his review of *Summoned by Bells* (1960), and in his much longer introduction to an American edition of the *Collected Poems* in 1971, we see Larkin's enthusiasm for Betjeman, his favourite contemporary poet, one 'for whom the modern poetic revolution has simply not taken place'; and learn that he does not read Betjeman uncritically, and is aware of the danger involved in the poet self-consciously turning himself into a 'personality': yet 'although it remains a mystery how Mr Betjeman can avoid the trap of self-importance, exhibitionism, silliness, sentimentality and boredom, he continues to do so'. Three of the essays deal with Hardy, and, in reply to 'the usual stuff' about not many of the poems meriting serious attention, he declares his wish to 'trumpet the assurance that one reader at least would not wish Hardy's *Collected Poems* a single page shorter, and regards it as many times over the best body of poetic work this century so far has to show'. His review of a new annotated Tennyson (1969) gives a very sympathetic but, again, not uncritical view of the poetry: he declares that 'it is pretty certain that the general reader would sooner be wrecked on a desert island with a complete Tennyson than with a complete Wordsworth' (although he elsewhere mentions Wordsworth – but not Tennyson – among his handful of favourite poets); he expresses some doubts about Tennyson's 'perfect ear', accepts without question the greatness of the lyrics and of 'In Memoriam', and singles out the 'anecdotal or dialect poems' for special commendation (there is also an enthusiastic essay on the most celebrated of English dialect poets, William Barnes). Many more of Larkin's enthusiasms find their way into *Required Writing*: Stevie Smith, Wilfred Owen, Edward Thomas, Anthony Powell, and Barbara Pym. His liking for Emily Dickinson is carefully, and revealingly, qualified: 'Her successes, when one comes to think of them, are when she is at her least odd, her most controlled. This is worth remembering in an age when almost any poet who can produce evidence of medical mental care is automatically ranked higher than one who has stayed sane.' Larkin clearly held to the end the critical credo of *New Lines*.

All these details come from the section called 'Writing in Particular'; and it is natural to go on from this to look at the essays on 'Writing in General', along with the two lengthy interviews, in which he clearly tries to give full and helpful answers, in order to find out what we can about Larkin's general view of poetry. But if we do this, we shall be pulled up short. 'I've never had "ideas" about poetry,' Larkin declared. 'To me it's always been a personal, almost physical release or solution to a complex pressure of needs' (*RW* 67). At times he showed great impatience with literary criticism, as when he was asked in an interview what he had learned from his study of Auden, Thomas, Yeats, and Hardy, and broke out in reply, 'Oh, for Christ's sake, one doesn't *study* poets! You *read* them' (*RW* 71). At other times, he indicated that theorizing about literature was fine as long as he didn't have to do it: asked to describe the genesis and working-out of a poem, he replied, 'If I could answer that sort of question, I'd be a professor rather than a librarian.'

All the same, Larkin did hold what could be called a theory of poetry, though he insisted that it should be thought of as a working hypothesis only ('I don't have to lecture,' he liked to say). He saw it as a way of preserving experience: 'it seems as if you've seen this sight, felt this feeling, had this vision, and have got to find a combination of words that will preserve it by setting it off in other people' (*RW* 58). The value of this act of preserving and communicating was, for Larkin, immense and irreplaceable: in his early twenties he declared that 'the only quality that makes art durable and famous is the quality of generating delight in the state of living' (*SL* 115) and he never changed this belief.

Larkin's dislike of modernism sprang from his belief that it had destroyed this quality of delight. He often described modernism as an 'aberration' that 'blighted all the arts', and claimed that he wrote poetry 'as everyone did, until the mad lads started, using words and syntax in the normal way, to describe recognizable experiences as memorably as possible' (*RW* 75). He could not forgive the 'mad lads' for making poetry wilfully difficult, for (as he saw it) interposing the need for commentators between poem and public. Larkin's fullest attack on modernism comes in the preface to *All What Jazz*, his collection of jazz reviews, where he attacks modernism 'not because it is new but because it is an irresponsible exploitation of technique in contradiction of human life as we know it. . . . It helps us neither to enjoy nor to endure' (*RW* 297).

The hostility to modernism went with a hostility to the academic study of literature. He believed that they supported each other: difficult texts demand teachers to explain them, and the existence of such teachers encourages difficulty:

> Universities have long been the accepted stamping ground for the subsidized acceptance of art rather than the real purchase of it – and so, of course, for . . . criticism designed to prevent people using their eyes and ears and understandings to report pleasure and discomfort. In such circumstances, modernism is bound to flourish. (*RW* 294).

Along with Larkin's rejection of modernism, indeed forming part of it, goes his rejection of foreign poetry, and of what he derisively called the 'myth-kitty' (*RW* 79). His lack of interest in foreign poetry was sometimes put with deliberate philistinism:

'if that chap Laforgue wants me to read his things, he'd better write them in English' (*SL* 274). But behind this crudeness there was a serious and thoughtful point, stated most vigorously in his *Paris Review* interview: 'I don't see how one can ever know a foreign language well enough to make reading poems in it worthwhile. . . . A writer can have only one language, if language is going to mean anything to him' (*RW* 69). Larkin disliked the view that poems are born from other poems, insisting that they must come from 'personal non-literary experience'. This is a strikingly Romantic statement, locating the source of a poem entirely in the poet's own experience, and it goes with Larkin's hostility to T. S. Eliot, the most celebrated modern defender of tradition, and to Dylan Thomas, whose poems are resonant with hints of myth. Larkin emerges from these statements as the typical Movement poet – matter of fact, contemporary, and direct in manner, rejecting pretentiousness, cloudy verbiage and learned allusions – the poet as ordinary man.

Such strongly expressed views must make the critic uneasy. The very idea of writing a book on Larkin seems to defy his own wishes; 'the only things one can do about literature', he wrote, 'are to write it, read it, or publish it: all this jaw is pure waste of time' (*SL* 314) – or, in an interview, 'When you've read a poem, that's it, it's all quite clear what it means' (*RW* 54). Yet it is surprising how often readers who agree in general terms that a poem is unambiguous find that they are reading the same poem differently; and critics are useful, too, because what poets say about their work does not always correspond to what they do. It is natural, then to ask if this was the case with Larkin. Some of these statements are clearly prompted by his rejection of his own early work. When he republished *The North Ship* in 1966, twenty-one years after its first appearance, he added a rather embarrassed preface ('the predominance of Yeats in this volume deserves some explanation'; 'this search for a style was merely one aspect of a general immaturity'); and one final poem of which he said that 'though not noticeably better than the rest, [it] shows the Celtic fever abated and the patient sleeping soundly' (*RW* 27–30). The cure for the Celtic fever, Larkin claimed, was provided by Thomas Hardy, and we owe to Larkin himself the division of his work into an early and modernist phase, dominated by Yeats, and the later, more mature phase, deriving from Hardy, consciously English, employing speech rhythms, and exploring contemporary situations.

Some of Larkin's most interesting critics, most notably Andrew Motion and Barbara Everett, have found this picture misleading, insisting that Larkin belongs much more firmly in the modernist movement than he liked to believe, linking him even with the French *Symbolistes* whom he claimed to despise and know little of (hence the connection between his anti-modernism and his dismissal of foreign poetry). There is some evidence that Larkin read more foreign poetry than he admitted: several references to French poetry occur in his notebooks, and there is, most interestingly, his poem 'Femmes Damnées', written in 1943 though not published until 1978. The title directs us to a poem by Baudelaire, describing two Lesbians, Hippoltye and Delphine, exploring their feelings after a sexual encounter in highly rhetorical speeches. Delphine, the older and more experienced, insists that her kisses are soft as mayflies, in contrast to those of a brutal male lover, which 'creuseront leurs ornières | Comme des chariots ou des socs déchirants' (will dig ruts, like wagons, or ploughshares which tear their way). Hippolyte, younger and deeply disturbed, declares that she is torn between love and guilt:

> Je frissonne de peur quand tu me dis: 'Mon ange!'
> Et cependant je sens ma bouche aller vers toi.
>
> (I shiver with fear when you say 'My angel!'
> But all the same I feel my mouth moving towards you)

but she surrenders to the caresses of Delphine, in which she finds the freshness of the tomb. The poem concludes with five stanzas in which the poet comments in his own voice:

> Descendez, descendez, lamentables victimes,
> Descendez le chemin de l'enfer éternel!...
>
> (Descend, descend, lamentable victims,
> Descend the path to everlasting hell!....

The moral condemnation in these concluding stanzas is so explicit that it is surprising to discover that 'Femmes damnées' was one of the poems that had to be removed from *Les Fleurs du mal* when the volume was judged to be obscene; clearly the addition of these moralizing remarks was not considered sufficient to make up for the explicit sexuality.

Larkin's version of this poem is much shorter (six stanzas instead of twenty-six) and very different in tone and style. Although Baudelaire's poem has a contemporary setting, it is impregnated with suggestions of the exotic and the mysterious: the women have Greek-sounding names, the lamps in the opening line 'languish', the cushions are steeped in odours. Larkin, in contrast, calls his women Rosemary and Rachel (even referring to the latter, in a detached, mocking, deliberately unpoetic tone, as 'Miss Rachel Wilson'); and the room is described through the kind of matter-of-fact, everyday details that carry the imprint of the later Larkin, but certainly not of Baudelaire: 'The milk's been on the step, | The *Guardian* in the letter-box, since dawn.' Only one stanza, the fifth, sounds like Baudelaire:

> Stretched out before her, Rachel curls and curves,
> Eyelids and lips apart, her glances filled
> With satisfied ferocity; she smiles,
> As beasts smile on the prey they have just killed.

Larkin not only omits the speeches in which the women explore their emotions with a polished savagery that suggests Racine; he also omits the concluding, moralizing stanzas, ending the poem simply with a sinister understatement: 'The only sound heard is the sound of tears.'

It is clear from this poem that the Larkin of 1943 was more interested in French poetry than he later admitted; but it is also clear that he went out of his way to domesticate and Anglicize Baudelaire's foreign eloquence. And there is one other interesting fact about 'Femmes Damnées': Larkin did not write the poem in his own person. When at Oxford he had invented a character called Brunette Coleman, under whose name he wrote a couple of unfinished, mildly erotic novels set in a girls' school, and also a number of poems. The invention of Brunette was intended as a joke (she was named after a band leader called Blanche Coleman) but at the same time she served as a persona for Larkin himself. 'Femmes Damnées' was attributed to Brunette as a way for Larkin to claim that the poem was not really 'by' him – whether because of the near-pornography (by the standards of 1943: it looks mild enough today) or because it is foreign poetry, we cannot say.

The presence of Baudelaire among the influences of Larkin's youth does not of course invalidate the orthodox view of his development (Hardy replacing Yeats), and the argument of Motion and Everett goes further, in its insistence on the symbolist elements in Larkin's mature poetry, and its claim that he never rejected modernism or abandoned Yeats as completely as he claimed. In order to judge this, it is necessary to pause a moment on the term 'symbolist'. Yeats's poetry, certainly, is full of symbols (so, after all, is most poetry); and it is true that the dominant figures in the modern movement were the French *symbolistes* (Rimbaud, Mallarmé, Laforgue, Valéry), but that does not necessarily mean that Yeats belongs with these poets. He began as a poet in the late Romantic tradition, and his early verse is full of symbols (rose, cloud, stars, moon) in a way reminiscent of Shelley or Rossetti: the break in his career that shifted him to being modern was a shift in style and linguistic register ('going naked', in his phrase), and the mature Yeats uses symbols rather less than the young Yeats. The sense in which the French modernists, on the other hand, are *symbolistes* (I shall write the word with an 'e', as in French, to make the distinction clear) derives from the belief that poetry is written (in Valéry's words) in 'a language within the language', and from their attempt to dispense with narrative and argument as organizing principles, consigning these to prose, and relying on the associations of words to unify their utterances. Yeats may be a poet who uses symbols, but he is not, in this sense, *symboliste*: the English language poets in that tradition are Eliot and Pound, Wallace Stevens, and Hart Crane. Larkin was well aware of all this when he said of his poem 'Absences': 'I fancy it sounds like a different, better poet than myself. The last line sounds like a slightly unconvincing translation from a French Symbolist[e]. I wish I could write like this more often.' The wonderful haunting quality of that last line – 'Such attics cleared of me! Such absences!' – derives not so much from the fact that an attic is a symbol of isolation (though it is) as from the way both the image (attic) and the abstract noun (absences) work in parallel to suggest the not fully articulated longing emerging from the contemplation of the seascape that the poem had up to then described. This is nothing like Yeats, but could certainly be taken

47

for Baudelaire, even Mallarmé. Even the apologetic 'sounds like a slightly unconvincing translation from' may not be mere modesty: it may record an awareness of the deliberate break-down of logic in *symboliste* poetry, the way in which some of its most moving lines may feel unconvincing if thought of as part of a total structure, yet may be all the more moving for that. Larkin, in fact, seems to be granting that there is some truth in the Motion–Everett case, but that it has little to do with Yeats, and is certainly not central to his mature work.

It might, therefore, be interesting to look in that work, not for the presence of Yeats (whom Larkin had loved), but for that of the unquestionably modernist Eliot (of whom he was often scornful). There are perhaps no English poems which show the influence of the French *symbolistes* as clearly as the four tiny townscapes that Eliot grouped together under the title 'Pre-ludes' (since the analogy between poetry and music is central to Valéry's poetic theory, the use of the musical analogy is itself a sign of *symboliste* influence). Here is one of them:

> The winter evening settles down
> With smell of steak in passageways.
> Six o'clock.
> The burnt-out ends of smoky days.
> And now a gusty shower wraps
> The grimy scraps
> Of withered leaves about your feet
> And newspapers from vacant lots;
> The showers beat
> On broken blinds and chimney pots,
> And at the corner of the street
> A lonely cab-horse steams and stamps.
>
> And then the lighting of the lamps.

How do we distinguish literal description from symbolic representation in this poem? There are details that one could actually observe on a winter evening, and there are formal similes (as, in a later 'Prelude', 'the worlds revolve like ancient women | Gathering fuel in vacant lots' – but that, too, is an observable detail, though transposed into a simile), and there are metaphors that attempt to convey the feeling associated with the scene, that it is drab ('The burnt-out ends of smoky days') or that it is frightening ('His soul stretched tight across the skies').

Since the vehicle of all the metaphors is taken from observed (or observable) details, it does not seem to matter much whether they are left as details or turned into figures of speech: the poem consists of a series of images whose quality remains much the same, all of which belong to the scene, but whose formal and logical status shifts.

Larkin wrote that kind of poetry too. Here is his 'Prelude':

FRIDAY NIGHT IN THE ROYAL STATION HOTEL

Light spreads darkly downwards from the high
Clusters of lights over empty chairs
That face each other, coloured differently.
Through open doors, the dining-room declares
A larger loneliness of knives and glass
And silence laid like carpet. A porter reads
An unsold evening paper. Hours pass,
And all the salesmen have gone back to Leeds,
Leaving full ashtrays in the Conference Room.

In shoeless corridors, the lights burn. How
Isolated, like a fort, it is –
The headed paper, made for writing home
(If home existed) letters of exile: *Now*
Night comes on. Waves fold behind villages.

This evening too settles down with smell of steak in passage-ways. In Larkin, as in Eliot, every detail is observable, so that, although the knives, forks, and carpets are, logically, present only as the vehicles of a comparison, they obviously belong as much to the hotel as the evening paper or the full ashtrays. (The only detail that does not, the fort, is surely the most conventional, least interesting touch in the poem.)

Eliot's 'Preludes' are in the bones of the reader of modern poetry: they form a kind of assumed basis for the language of poetry, showing that it can be about city life, and that it can use images as the direct representation of emotion – as the poet openly says at one point: 'I am moved by fancies that are curled | Around these images'. And, despite Larkin's anti-modernism, the 'Preludes' seem to be in his bones too; and in this poem he has even gone one better than his master. The early Eliot, we all know, is the poet of alienation; and how elegantly Larkin skirts that word in the last three lines. And the two italicized sentences, which are (presumably) part of the 'letter of exile', also state the method of the poem. Philip Larkin sits in the hotel writing-room after dinner and uses the hotel writing paper to start sketching a poem about the local scenery, a poem which is also a statement about alienation. Or rather, he does not – but he might, and if he did, that is what he would write on the headed paper. The poem declares itself to be an act of writing, it is what might be written if. It seems incredible to claim for plain blunt Larkin a greater degree of sophistication than for old Possum himself, but it is almost as if we have here, to use Barthes's well-known terminology, a *scriptible* (or writerly) rather than a *lisible* (readerly) text, one that says to the reader, If you were here, this is what you might be tempted to write.

Larkin's poetry can be seen as moving between two extremes. On the one hand, there is the wry, ironic voice of the poet as ordinary man, bored and ignorant in church, removing his cycle clips in awkward reverence: this is the aspect of his work that has made him famous, that predominates in his finest poems, and that has been stressed in this book; on the other hand, there is the element that has appealed so strongly to some of his fellow poets and his more sophisticated critics, the 'repining for a more crystalline reality' (the words are Seamus Heaney's in his essay 'The Main of Light'), the emphasis on absence, forgetting, and emptiness. 'The Winter Palace', one of his very last poems, unpublished until it appeared in the *Collected Poems*, is entirely about forgetting: it moves from a vague grumbling at how the passing years cause him to forget more and more to a conclusion that celebrates oblivion:

> Then there will be nothing I know.
> My mind will fold into itself, like fields, like snow.

– or, to put this in terms of recent literary theory, he will inhabit a world of pure signifiers.

Does this mean that Larkin came full circle, returning after all to the visionary, Yeatsian writing of his early work?

> When waves fling loudly
> And fall at the stern
> I am wakened each dawn
> Increasingly to fear
> Salt-stiffening air,
> The birdless sea.
>
> . . . . .

Seventy feet down
The sea explodes upwards,
Relapsing, to slaver
Off landing-stage steps –
Running suds, rejoice!

Twenty-seven years separate these two passages, so similar and yet so different. The first, from '65° N' was written in 1944 and appeared in *The North Ship* (see *CP* 303), a volume which would be forgotten today if it were not for Larkin's later work; the second, from 'Livings II', was written in 1971, and appeared in *High Windows*, perhaps the most admired volume of post-war poetry. Is the second really so much finer than the first? It is better written, certainly (there is nothing so felicitous as 'slaver' in the first), but not obviously so; the emotional contrast (the first expressing fear, the second exhilaration) is untypical, since fear is so much more prominent in the later Larkin. Only by placing the passages in their context can we see how different they really are. The speaker of the first is looking within and using an image for what he finds there; the second is literal: the speaker is actually watching a rough sea. The first passage is spoken by the poet himself; the second is attributed to a persona, and forms part of a sequence of three poems about contrasting ways of life (this speaker is evidently a lighthouse keeper). And the first is not noticeably different from anything else in *The North Ship*, whereas the second emerges in sharp contrast to the poems around it. For the most important breakthrough in Larkin's poetic development was the move *towards* the timid, reasonable ordinariness that Heaney likes to see him shedding, towards the disillusioned man strolling down Cemetery Road, hating home with its specially chosen junk, setting his sights no higher than finding 'Words at once true and kind, | Or not untrue and not unkind.' When a visionary moment appears in *High Windows*, it has thrust its way in among this other, very different writing. Larkin illustrated better than any other contemporary poet what we can call the apple-pie principle, that apple pie is nicer than apple, but the nicest part of the apple pie is the apple. Larkin's visionary gleam is the finest thing in many of the poems, but we value it more fully when we find it in the crusty context of the voice complaining 'I detest my room... | And my life, in perfect order.'

51

I have already tried to show how this is true of 'High Windows'; in conclusion, we can see how it applies to 'Sad Steps', another late poem that seems to step into and out of modernism. Its title is a literary allusion (to Philip Sidney's sonnet about the moon) of the kind Larkin often objected to; it begins with the familiar Larkin coarseness ('Groping back to bed after a piss...'), and then describes with great vividness the moon in the night sky,

> High and preposterous and separate –
> Lozenge of love! Medallion of art!
> O wolves of memory! Immensements!...

These two lines sound just like 'a slightly unconvincing translation from a French symbolist'. It is striking that they consist of exclamations: the modernist elements in the later Larkin often make use of exclamatory sentences, for such a sentence structure, with its absence of verbs, obviously fits the attempt to reach beyond language, an awareness that the sight of the moon evokes something that cannot be coherently articulated. 'High Windows' ended on that note, but 'Sad Steps' reverts to the prosaic:

> O wolves of memory! Immensements! No,
>
> One shivers slightly, looking up there.
> The hardness and the brightness and the plain
> Far-reaching singleness of that wide stare
>
> Is a reminder of the strength and pain
> Of being young: that it can't come again,
> But is for others undiminished somewhere.

The 'No' at the end of that line is a brilliant switch of register, denying the extravagant modernist gesture of the preceding image, returning us to the embarrassed voice of the middle-aged man who refers to himself as 'one'. And the poem ends as 'Church Going' ended: just as the secular, unbelieving tourist had to confront the deep meaningfulness of the churches that others had built, so the middle-aged, self-deprecating Larkin cannot surrender himself to the transfiguring beauty of the moon, but knows that it is 'for others undiminished somewhere'. Beauty must give place to truth, but the truth is that beauty will always proffer itself.

Select Bibliography

WORKS BY LARKIN

Collected Poems, ed. Anthony Thwaite (London: Faber & Faber and the Marvell Press, 1988). Contains all four of Larkin's published volumes, besides all the unpublished poems of his maturity that the editor considered to be finished, and a selection of juvenilia. It is the only book needed by those who wish to read Larkin's poetry. (Publication details of the original volumes of poetry are given in the Biographical Outline.)

Jill (London: Fortune Press, 1946; new edn., Faber & Faber, 1975).

A Girl in Winter (London: Faber & Faber, 1947).

All What Jazz: A Record Diary 1961–8 (London: Faber & Faber, 1970).

Required Writing: Miscellaneous Pieces 1955–1982 (London: Faber & Faber, 1983). Contains all Larkin's critical prose of any importance.

Selected Letters of Philip Larkin 1940–1985, ed. Anthony Thwaite (London: (Faber & Faber, 1992).

EDITED BY LARKIN

The Oxford Book of Twentieth Century English Verse (Oxford: Oxford University Press, 1973).

BIBLIOGRAPHY

Bloomfield, B. C., *Philip Larkin: A Bibliography, 1933–1976* (London: Faber & Faber, 1979). This work is very thorough, and, since Larkin published so little after 1976, can be regarded as almost complete.

BIOGRAPHY

Motion, Andrew, *Philip Larkin: A Writer's Life* (London: Faber & Faber, 1993). This very full biography by a friend of Larkin's, who spent many hours interviewing those who knew him, renders other biographical studies unnecessary, and is virtually certain never to be replaced.

Bennett, Alan, 'Alas! Deceived', *London Review of Books*, 25 March 1993. Motion's biography prompted several long and valuable reviews, of which this is probably the best.

Booth, James, *Philip Larkin, Writer* (Hemel Hempstead: Harvester Wheatsheaf, 1992). Chapter 1 is the best short account of Larkin's life (containing some material not in Motion).

CRITICISM

Now that Larkin has become, after Betjeman, the most popular English poet of the later 20th century, there is a flood of introductions to and expositions of his poetry, and some of the most useful are noted below. Because so much of Larkin's poetry hovers delicately between making and undercutting assertions, between trusting statement and trusting imagery, it is inevitable that critics will differ in their readings; and to read too many of them (as the compiler of a reading list necessarily must) is to long for the immediacy of the poems themselves.

Larkin criticism is perhaps as interesting for what it tells us about the culture we live in as it is for helping us to read the poetry. Much recent Larkin criticism is tendentious, maintaining a theoretical or political position from which the poems are viewed and, often, judged. Three overlapping tendencies can be discerned. First, those elements in Larkin's personal life which are (to put it kindly) unfashionable, or (to put it harshly) misogynistic, racist or reactionary, have entered more and more into discussion, so that he is widely known as a foul-mouthed bigot to those who had read little of his poetry. With this view I have no sympathy (see p. 25). Second, there have been attempts, in defiance of Larkin's own assertions, to see him as a modernist: this is most powerfully argued by Andew Motion and Barbara Everett. And third, those critics who belive strongly that poetry is not for all time but of an age have insisted on relating Larkin to attitudes and tendencies in late 20th century Britain: the most powerful voices here are Stephen Regan and Tom Paulin, and the approach is explicitly argued about in the controversy between Regan and Booth in *Larkin with Poetry*.

BOOKS ON LARKIN

Booth, James, *Philip Larkin, Writer* (Hemel Hempstead: Harvester Wheatsheaf, 1992). Attacks all didactic and reductive readings of Larkin, and contains some of the most careful and subtle (sometimes perhaps oversubtle) discussions of his technique.

Brownjohn, Alan, *Philip Larkin* (Harlow: Longman for the British Council, 1975). A useful volume in 'Writers and their Work', the previous version of the present series.

Cookson, Linda, and Loughrey, Bryan (eds.), *Philip Larkin: The Poems* (London: Longmans, 1989). Aimed specifically at students: consists mostly of discussion of particular poems. The liveliest essay (by Graham Holderness, contrasting him with Dylan Thomas) is also the least sympathetic to Larkin.

Day, Roger, *Philip Larkin* (Milton Keynes: Open University Press, 1976). This is Unit 28 of the Open University course on Twentieth Century Poetry, and, as is normal with the Open University, is written in question and answer form, designed as an instrument for teaching. It consists almost entirely of discussions of actual poems.

Morrison, Blake, *The Movement: English Poetry and Fiction of the 1950s* (Oxford: Oxford University Press, 1980). The most thorough, scholarly, and judicious account of the literary movement to which, it maintains, Larkin, despite his disclaimers, clearly belongs.

Motion, Andrew, *Philip Larkin* (London: Methuen, 1982). Claims that Larkin's poetry is more modernist than he, and most critics, have admitted. 'The Hardyesque languages of isolation and sadness are constantly negotiating in his poems with the Yeatsian languages of aspiration and transcendence.'

Petch, Simon, *The Art of Philip Larkin* (Sydney: Sydney University Press, 1981). Careful analyses of most of the poems, laying great emphasis on the idea of persona.

Regan, Stephen, *Philip Larkin* (London: Macmillan, 1992). Designed as 'an introduction to the variety of criticism', this book argues strongly, even aggressively, for the superiority of 'historicist' over other critical approaches.

Swarbrick, Andrew, *Out of Reach: The Poetry of Philip Larkin* (London: Macmillan, 1995). Very thorough and detailed study, with a strong biographical slant, moving constantly between the poems and the poet.

Timms, David, *Philip Larkin* (Edinburgh: Oliver & Boyd, 1973). Unpretentious and helpful: perhaps the best introduction to Larkin.

Tolley, A. T., *My Proper Ground: A Study of the Work of Philip Larkin and its Development* (Edinburgh University Press, 1991). Thorough and balanced. 'His denials (that anything may be held on to or reached back to) seem only to make the gestures more poignant.'

Whalen, Terry, *Philip Larkin and English Poetry* (London: Macmillan, 1986). Attempts to place Larkin in an 'imagist' tradition; relates him to Dr Johnson, to Lawrence, and to Ted Hughes.

Collections of essays

Baron, Michael (ed.), *Larkin with Poetry* (English Association, 1997). Contains Stephen Regan's defence of historicist placing of Larkin ('Larkin's Reputation') and James Booth's attack on this approach ('Philip Larkin: Lyricism, Englishness and Postcoloniality').

Booth, James (ed.), *New Larkins for Old* (London: Macmillan, 2000). Gathers together some of the liveliest recent critics of Larkin.

Salwak, Dale (ed.), *Philip Larkin: The Man and his Work* (London: Macmillan, 1989).

Thwaite, Anthony (ed.), *Larkin at Sixty* (London: Faber & Faber, 1982).

Phoenix, 11, 12 (Autumn and Winter 1973–4): Philip Larkin issue.

Critical Survey, 1/2 (1989): Larkin issue.

ARTICLES

Ackroyd, Peter, 'Poet Hands on Misery to Man', *The Times*, 1 April 1993. Discussed in Chapter 4.

Crawford, Robert, *Devolving English Literature* (Oxford: Oxford University Press, 1992), 271–7. Relates Larkin's poetry to the idea of Englishness.

Davie, Donald, 'Landscapes of Larkin', in *Thomas Hardy and British Poetry* (London: Routledge, 1973), 63–82. For Larkin 'there is to be no historical perspective, no measuring of present against past': he is Hardy's heir, but 'sells off a great deal of his inherited estate'. A boldly argued view of the political implications of Larkin's humanism.

Everett, Barbara, 'Philip Larkin: After Symbolism', *Essays in Criticism*, 30 (1980), 227–42. Beginning from an interpretation of 'Sympathy in White Major' as a learned poem, deriving from, and even about, Gautier and Mallarmé, locates Larkin's poetry (despite his denials) in the French *symboliste* tradition.

—— 'Larkin's Edens', *English*, 31 (1982), 41–53.

—— 'Art and Larkin', in Dale Salwak (ed.), *Philip Larkin: The Man and his Work* (London: Macmillan, 1989), 129–39. Praises Larkin's poetry because, without being Philistine, 'it made itself vulnerable to the charge that it was'.

Falck, Colin, 'Philip Larkin', *The Review*, 14 (Dec. 1964), 3–11; repr. in

Twentieth Century Poetry: Critical Essays and Documents, ed. Graham Martin and P. N. Furbank (Milton Keynes: Open University Press, 1975). A tendentious, vigorous, rather Lawrentian attempt to discriminate between the elements in Larkin that 'point ultimately to a dead end' and those that can 'bring our dreams into relation to reality'.

Heaney, Seamus, 'Englands of the Mind' (1976), in *Preoccupations: Selected Prose 1968–78* (London: Faber & Faber, 1980), 150–69.

—— 'The Main of Light' (1982), in Anthony Thwaite (ed.), *Larkin at Sixty* (London: Faber & Faber, 1982), 131–8. Sensitive examinations of Larkin's technique by the Nobel Laureate.

James, Clive, 'Somewhere Becoming Rain', *New Yorker*, 17 July 1989. Excellent review of the *Collected Poems*, noting how carefully Larkin arranged the poems in each volume.

Jardine, Lisa, 'Saxon Violence', *Guardian*, 8 December 1992. Discussed in Chapter 4.

King, P. R., 'Philip Larkin', in *Nine Contemporary Poets* (London: Methuen, 1979). A useful introductory essay.

Longley, Edna, 'Any-Angled Light: Philip Larkin and Edward Thomas', in her *Poetry in the Wars* (Newcastle upon Tyne: Bloodaxe Books, 1986). Relentlessly thorough comparison of Larkin with a poet he admired; discusses their common Englishness, their use of non-human nature when writing about people, their 'combination of nostalgia, desire and death-wish', their agnosticism, their metrical techniques. Both write poems 'to preserve things'.

—— 'Larkin, Decadence and the Lyric Poem' in *New Larkins for Old* (above). Edna Longley's dense style, her psycho-analytic interests, and her habit of leaping from poem to poem make her difficult to read, but she is one of the subtlest contemporary critics of poetry.

Nye, Robert, 'Poetry of Furnished Rooms', *The Times*, 20 October 1988. Intelligent and discriminating review of the *Collected Poems*.

Paulin, Tom, 'Philip Larkin' in *Minotaur: Poetry & the Nation State* (London: Faber & Faber, 1992). Intelligent and provocative discussion of the 'connection between the personal and the national life' in Larkin's poems, which are described as 'public statements disguised as lyric poems'.

Pritchard, William H., 'Larkin's Presence', in Dale Salwak (ed.), *Philip Larkin: The Man and his Work* (London: Macmillan, 1989), 71–89. Lively, personal and scholarly, full of perceptive insights; one of the best general essays on Larkin's poetry.

Wain, John, 'The Poetry of Philip Larkin', in *Professing Poetry* (London: Macmillan, 1977), 160–80. Informal appreciation of Larkin's poetry, with very perceptive comments on particular poems. Aware of 'the difficulty of saying what Larkin writes "about"', but has no doubt that the subjects of the poem are important.

Watson, J. R., 'The Other Larkin', *Critical Quarterly*, 17 (Winter) 1975, 347–60. Beneath the surface of the careful painting of provincial middle-class England, there is another Larkin, who celebrates 'the unexpressed, deeply-felt longings for sacred time and sacred space'.

—— 'Philip Larkin: Voices and Values' in Dale Salwak (ed.), *Philip Larkin: The Man and his Work* (London: Macmillan, 1989), 90–111. Relates the voice of Larkin the man, especially as heard in his recorded readings, to the tone and rhythm of the poems.

Index

*Recent and
Forthcoming Titles
in the
New Series of*

WRITERS AND
THEIR WORK

WRITERS AND THEIR WORK

RECENT & FORTHCOMING TITLES

Title	Author
William Golding 2/e	*Kevin McCarron*
Graham Greene	*Peter Mudford*
Neil M. Gunn	*J. B. Pick*
Ivor Gurney	*John Lucas*
Hamlet 2/e	*Ann Thompson & Neil Taylor*
Thomas Hardy 2/e	*Peter Widdowson*
Tony Harrison	*Joe Kelleher*
William Hazlitt	*J. B. Priestley; R. L. Brett (intro. by Michael Foot)*
Seamus Heaney 2/e	*Andrew Murphy*
George Herbert	*T.S. Eliot (intro. by Peter Porter)*
Geoffrey Hill	*Andrew Roberts*
Gerard Manley Hopkins	*Daniel Brown*
Henrik Ibsen 2/e	*Sally Ledger*
Kazuo Ishiguro 2/e	*Cynthia Wong*
Henry James – The Later Writing	*Barbara Hardy*
James Joyce 2/e	*Steven Connor*
Julius Caesar	*Mary Hamer*
Franz Kafka	*Michael Wood*
John Keats	*Kelvin Everest*
James Kelman	*Gustav Klaus*
Hanif Kureishi	*Ruvani Ranasinha*
Samuel Johnson	*Liz Bellamy*
William Langland: *Piers Plowman*	*Claire Marshall*
King Lear	*Terence Hawkes*
Philip Larkin 2/e	*Laurence Lerner*
D. H. Lawrence	*Linda Ruth Williams*
Doris Lessing	*Elizabeth Maslen*
C. S. Lewis	*William Gray*
Wyndham Lewis and Modernism	*Andrzej Gasiorak*
David Lodge	*Bernard Bergonzi*
Katherine Mansfield	*Andrew Bennett*
Christopher Marlowe	*Thomas Healy*
Andrew Marvell	*Annabel Patterson*
Ian McEwan 2/e	*Kiernan Ryan*
Measure for Measure	*Kate Chedgzoy*
The Merchant of Venice	*Warren Chernaik*
A Midsummer Night's Dream	*Helen Hackett*
Alice Munro	*Ailsa Cox*
Vladimir Nabokov	*Neil Cornwell*
V. S. Naipaul	*Suman Gupta*
Grace Nichols	*Sarah Lawson-Welsh*
Edna O'Brien	*Amanda Greenwood*
Flann O'Brien	*Joe Brooker*
Ben Okri	*Robert Fraser*
George Orwell	*Douglas Kerr*
Othello	*Emma Smith*
Walter Pater	*Laurel Brake*
Brian Patten	*Linda Cookson*
Caryl Phillips	*Helen Thomas*
Harold Pinter	*Mark Batty*
Sylvia Plath 2/e	*Elisabeth Bronfen*
Pope Amongst the Satirists	*Brean Hammond*

TITLES IN PREPARATION

Title	Author
Fleur Adcock	*Janet Wilson*
Ama Ata Aidoo	*Nana Wilson-Tagoe*
Matthew Arnold	*Kate Campbell*
Margaret Atwood	*Marion Wynne-Davies*
John Banville	*Peter Dempsey*
William Barnes	*Christopher Ricks*
Black British Writers	*Deidre Osborne*
William Blake	*Steven Vine*
Charlotte Brontë	*Stevie Davies*
Robert Browning	*John Woodford*
Basil Bunting	*Martin Stannard*
John Bunyan	*Tamsin Spargoe*
Children's Writers of the 19th Century	*Mary Sebag-Montefiore*
Coriolanus	*Anita Pacheco*
Cymbeline	*Peter Swaab*
Douglas Dunn	*David Kennedy*
David Edgar	*Peter Boxall*
T. S. Eliot	*Colin MacCabe*
J. G. Farrell	*John McLeod*
Nadine Gordimer	*Lewis Nkosi*
Geoffrey Grigson	*R. M. Healey*
David Hare	*Jeremy Ridgman*
Ted Hughes	*Susan Bassnett*
The Imagist Poets	*Andrew Thacker*
Ben Jonson	*Anthony Johnson*
A. L. Kennedy	*Dorothy McMillan*
Jack Kerouac	*Michael Hrebebiak*
Jamaica Kincaid	*Susheila Nasta*
Rudyard Kipling	*Jan Montefiore*
Rosamond Lehmann	*Judy Simon*
Una Marson & Louise Bennett	*Alison Donnell*
Norman MacCaig	*Alasdair Macrae*
Thomas Middleton	*Hutchings & Bromham*
John Milton	*Nigel Smith*
Much Ado About Nothing	*John Wilders*
R. K. Narayan	*Shirley Chew*
New Woman Writers	*Marion Shaw/Lyssa Randolph*
Ngugi wa Thiong'o	*Brendon Nicholls*
Religious Poets of the 17th Century	*Helen Wilcox*
Samuel Richardson	*David Deeming*
Olive Schreiner	*Carolyn Burdett*
Sam Selvon	*Ramchand & Salick*
Olive Senior	*Denise de Canes Narain*
Mary Shelley	*Catherine Sharrock*
Charlotte Smith & Helen Williams	*Angela Keane*
Ian Crichton Smith	*Colin Nicholson*
R. L. Stevenson	*David Robb*
Tom Stoppard	*Nicholas Cadden*
Elizabeth Taylor	*N. R. Reeve*
Dylan Thomas	*Chris Wiggington*
Three Avant-Garde Poets	*Peter Middleton*
Three Lyric Poets	*William Rowe*

TITLES IN PREPARATION

Title	Author
Derek Walcott	*Stephen Regan*
Jeanette Winterson	*Gina Vitello*
Women's Poetry at the Fin de Siècle	*Anna Vadillo*
William Wordsworth	*Nicola Trott*